School Counseling and School Social Work Homework Planner, Second Edition

Wiley Practice*Planners*®

Arthur E. Jongsma Jr., Series Editor

School Counseling and School Social Work Homework Planner

Second Edition

Sarah Edison Knapp

WILEY

Published by John Wiley & Sons, Inc., Hoboken, New Jersey
Published simultaneously in Canada

For general information about our other products and services, please contact our Customer Care Department within the United States at (800) 762-2974, outside the United States at (317) 572-3993 or fax (317) 572-4002.

Wiley publishes in a variety of print and electronic formats and by print-on-demand. Some material included with standard print versions of this book may not be included in e-books or in print-on-demand. If this book refers to media such as a CD or DVD that is not included in the version you purchased, you may download this material at http://booksupport.wiley.com. For more information about Wiley products, visit www.wiley.com.

Library of Congress Cataloging-in-Publication Data:

Knapp, Sarah Edison.
  School counseling and school social work homework planner / Sarah Edison Knapp. — Second edition.
    pages cm
  ISBN 978-1-119-38476-2 (paper)
  ISBN 978-1-119-38477-9 (epub)
  ISBN 978-1-119-38478-6 (ePDF)
  1. Educational counseling. 2. School social work. I. Title.
  LB1027.5.K587 2013
  371.4'22—dc23
                        2012046821

Printed in the United States of America

10 9 8 7 6 5 4 3 2 1

CONTENTS

WILEY PRACTICE*PLANNERS*® SERIES PREFACE

Accountability is an important dimension of the practice of psychotherapy. Treatment programs, public agencies, clinics, and practitioners must justify and document their treatment plans to outside review entities in order to be reimbursed for services. The books and software in the Wiley Practice*Planners*® series are designed to help practitioners fulfill these documentation requirements efficiently and professionally.

The Wiley Practice*Planners*® series includes a wide array of treatment planning books, including not only the original *Complete Adult Psychotherapy Treatment Planner*, *Child Psychotherapy Treatment Planner*, and *Adolescent Psychotherapy Treatment Planner*, all now in their fourth editions, but also *Treatment Planners* targeted to specialty areas of practice, such as:

- Addictions
- Co-occurring disorders
- Behavioral medicine
- College students
- Couples therapy
- Crisis counseling
- Early childhood education
- Employee assistance
- Family therapy
- Gays and lesbians
- Group therapy
- Juvenile justice and residential care
- Mental retardation and developmental disability
- Neuropsychology
- Older adults
- Parenting skills
- Pastoral counseling
- Personality disorders
- Probation and parole
- Psychopharmacology
- Rehabilitation psychology
- School counseling and school social work
- Severe and persistent mental illness
- Sexual abuse victims and offenders
- Social work and human services
- Special education

- Speech-language pathology
- Suicide and homicide risk assessment
- Veterans and active military duty
- Women's issues

In addition, three branches of companion books can be used in conjunction with the *Treatment Planners*, or on their own:

- ***Progress Notes Planners*** provide a menu of progress statements that elaborate on the client's symptom presentation and the provider's therapeutic intervention. Each *Progress Notes Planner* statement is directly integrated with the behavioral definitions and therapeutic interventions from its companion *Treatment Planner*.

- ***Homework Planners*** include homework assignments designed around each presenting problem (such as anxiety, depression, chemical dependence, anger management, eating disorders, or panic disorder) that is the focus of a chapter in its corresponding *Treatment Planner*.

- ***Client Education Handout Planners*** provide brochures and handouts to help educate and inform clients on presenting problems and mental health issues, as well as life skills techniques. The handouts are included online for easy printing from your computer and are ideal for use in waiting rooms, at presentations, as newsletters, or as information for clients struggling with mental illness issues. The topics covered by these handouts correspond to the presenting problems in the *Treatment Planners*.

Adjunctive books, such as *The Psychotherapy Documentation Primer* and *The Clinical Documentation Sourcebook*, contain forms and resources to aid clinicians in mental health practice management.

The goal of our series is to provide practitioners with the resources they need in order to provide high-quality care in the era of accountability. To put it simply: We seek to help you spend more time on patients and less time on paperwork.

ARTHUR E. JONGSMA, JR.
Grand Rapids, Michigan

ACKNOWLEDGMENTS

Many thanks to Dr. Arthur Jongsma, the series editor and co-author of the treatment planners that have helped hundreds of thousands of therapists in numerous treatment settings. *The School Counseling and School Social Work Treatment* and *Homework Planners* are a much-needed addition to the planner series and are now available because of Dr. Jongsma's foresight, dedication, and diligence. I often wish that I had these useful therapeutic guides while I was working with students in the schools. Thanks also to Sweta Gupta of John Wiley & Sons for her guidance and encouragement throughout the production process. Finally, thank you to my children, Michael Knapp, Jr. and Heather Werkema, for their love, encouragement, good humor, and insight that helped me survive and enjoy the time and effort it took to create this Homework Planner.

INTRODUCTION

School counselors and school social workers are seeing more and more students with varied and difficult issues to manage and overcome. The role of the school-based therapist is to assist the student and his or her teachers and family members in solving the problems that interfere with the student's successful adjustment to school and to life in general. Homework assignments and activities used in individual and group counseling sessions help the student invest in the therapeutic process and take responsibility for the effort necessary to reach the treatment goals.

The homework activities provided in this planner are designed to enhance the therapeutic interventions described in *The School Counseling and School Social Work Treatment Planner, Second Edition* (Knapp, Jongsma, & Dimmitt, 2012). Assessment tools are provided for use by the therapist, along with self-monitoring exercises for the student and numerous activities that can be completed by the student. These exercises can be assigned as a part of the counseling session or as homework between sessions to reinforce the insights and information processed during the individual or group sessions.

The homework activities presented in this planner speed up the attainment of therapeutic goals. Through the completion of assignments, the student becomes increasingly aware of the process of problem solving and the behavioral changes necessary to reach therapeutic goals. The activities help the student to clarify his or her issues of conflict and detrimental behavior patterns. They also empower the student to become actively involved in attaining socioemotional health. The insight gained as a result of the completed homework can be discussed during subsequent counseling sessions and used as a basis for more productive, successful behavioral and thought patterns.

During my 25 years as a school social worker, I used numerous written and interactive activities to enhance the therapeutic process with students of all ages and with varied socioemotional problems. Creating these activities was labor-intensive and time-consuming. *The School Counseling and School Social Work Homework Planner, Second Edition* provides 75 homework activities that are ready for you to copy and use with your students. This book will eliminate hours spent preparing activities for your ever-increasing caseload of students with a wide range of therapeutic issues.

USING THIS HOMEWORK PLANNER WITH STUDENTS

Homework activities help the student take the therapeutic process seriously and recognize his or her essential part in creating change. All of the activities are designed to be interesting and fun for the student, as well as helpful in resolving therapeutic issues. However, homework may have a negative connotation to students who already feel overwhelmed by the amount of assignments that they are required to complete for their academic classes. For the student who is reluctant to complete additional assignments, it will be helpful to have him or her begin the homework activity during the counseling session and to spend time discussing how the assignment will benefit him or her. Each exercise should be processed during the next counseling session to reinforce the value of the exercise and to acknowledge the student's time and effort spent completing it. If the homework is not complete, time for completion can be taken during the session and reasons for lack of completion can be discussed. This process will help the school-based therapist understand the student and how he or she deals with tasks and assignments more fully.

Many of the activities can be completed as part of the student's counseling sessions and will facilitate dialogue on the particular issues considered. The activities are designed to be used with the student individually or as part of a counseling group. Some require assistance from either the classroom teacher or the parents. The activities help the teacher or parent assist the student in dealing with classroom or at-home issues. It is wise to contact the teacher or parent to explain the activity and its intention and enlist their cooperation before you assign it to the student.

ABOUT THE ASSIGNMENTS

Two or more assignments correlate directly with each treatment concern presented in *The School Counseling and School Social Work Treatment Planner, Second Edition* (Knapp, Jongsma, & Dimmitt, 2012). These assignments are cited as part of the therapeutic interventions recommended for each identified problem in the Treatment Planner. Each exercise begins with a Counselor's Overview, which cites goals of the exercise, additional homework that may be applicable to the problem, additional problems for which the exercise may be useful, and suggestions for using the exercise with the student(s). These assignments are ready to be copied and used with your students. Each activity provides instructions for the student or students; however, in most cases these instructions should be covered and clarified during the counseling session. Not all homework activities are applicable to all students; your professional judgment should be used in assigning them, and often activities from other sections of this Homework Planner will be applicable to a presenting problem. All of the assignments can be tailored to fit the individual circumstances and needs of the student or group by using the word-processing disk that accompanies this Homework Planner. The therapist should feel free to alter the activities to best suit the requirements of the student and the issues addressed.

It is recommended that the therapist read through the entire book to become familiar with the activities that may be helpful to students. A suggested age range for appropriate use of the activity is given in most cases, but many of the activities can be modified slightly to suit students of various ages. If the student is being seen for several sessions or for an extended period, the activities can be kept in a therapeutic journal or notebook for easy reference and review. This journal or notebook will become a record of progress made during the counseling process and should be given to the student upon termination of the sessions.

The activities in *The School Counseling and School Social Work Homework Planner, Second Edition* are designed to accompany the therapeutic counseling process and should not be used independently without the guidance of a school-based therapist.

SARAH EDISON KNAPP

GOOD NEWS AND BAD NEWS OF MAKING IT IN SCHOOL

GOALS OF THE EXERCISE

1. Recognize that all behavior has consequences.
2. Identify the unconscious goals of underachievement.
3. Identify the hidden fears of achievement.
4. Establish strategies necessary to attain future goals.

ADDITIONAL PROBLEMS FOR WHICH THIS EXERCISE MAY BE MOST USEFUL

- Attention-Deficit/Hyperactivity Disorder (ADHD)
- Attention-Seeking Behavior
- Career Planning
- Responsible Behavior Training
- Oppositional Defiant Disorder (ODD)

SUGGESTIONS FOR USING THIS EXERCISE WITH STUDENT(S)

Every action has consequences. Behaviors that are repeated have consequences that make students feel better or validate their internal view of the world. Many actions have both positive and negative consequences; for instance, skipping a day of school (a strategy for underachievement) may give the student time to relax and watch TV (positive consequences) but also create more work to be completed upon his or her return to school and additional frustration trying to keep up with class discussions (negative consequences). The student who uses a successful school strategy (e.g., working for high grades) may feel a sense of accomplishment, be recognized by teachers and parents, and viewed by peers as smart (positive consequences) but may have higher expectations imposed, be viewed by peers as nerdy, and may have to do more work to maintain a high level of performance (negative consequences).

This activity will help the student recognize the reinforcing consequences of his or her behavior, the unconscious goals of underachievement, and the underlying fears of achievement. Once the reinforcing consequences are identified, the student will be free to determine if current self-defeating behaviors are likely to achieve his or her long-term goals and future expectations. Positive strategies for achievement can then be substituted for strategies that currently contribute to underachievement.

GOOD NEWS AND BAD NEWS OF MAKING IT IN SCHOOL

All behaviors have consequences. Responsible behavior in school helps you successfully complete assignments, achieve better grades, and make progress toward your future goals. Irresponsible behavior in school results in lack of knowledge and failure to reach your long-term goals. However, each behavior has some positive and some negative effects; for instance, although paying attention and raising your hand to participate results in increased knowledge and positive relationships with your classmates and teacher, this self-control takes time and effort. When you weigh the positive and the negative effects of your current behavior, you will be able to determine whether your actions contribute to or detract from the results you want to achieve.

Review the following list of strategies for personal and school achievement and underachievement and add some of your own ideas or strategies. Brainstorm the positive (Good News) and negative (Bad News) consequences of each strategy and record your ideas. Analyze your behavior and compare the strategies you use now to the strategies you will need for meeting your short- and long-term goals.

Strategies for Personal Achievement	Good News	Bad News
Raising my hand in class:	*Teacher appreciates my self-control.*	*I have to wait my turn.*
Listening to instructions:	*I know what I'm supposed to do.*	*I don't get to fool around in class.*

Write the good news and bad news consequences for each strategy.

Doing my homework:	_____	_____
Attending school regularly:	_____	_____
Studying for an exam:	_____	_____
Participating in class discussions:	_____	_____
Asking the teacher for help:	_____	_____
Getting tutoring:	_____	_____

Working with a mentor: _____ _____

Getting an A: _____ _____

Testing out in math: _____ _____

Taking accelerated classes: _____ _____

Belonging to an academic club: _____ _____

College acceptance: _____ _____

Getting a good job: _____ _____

_____ _____ _____

_____ _____ _____

_____ _____ _____

Strategies for Underachievement	Good News	Bad News
Skipping school:	*A day of leisure*	*More work to complete at school*

Write the good news and bad news consequences for each strategy.

Forgetting homework: _____ _____

Not participating in class: _____ _____

Daydreaming: _____ _____

Being a couch potato or video-game nerd: _____ _____

Being tardy for class: _____ _____

Refusing help from the teacher: _____ _____

_____ _____ _____

_____ _____ _____

_____ _____ _____

_____ _____ _____

_____ _____ _____

**Strategies I Am
Currently Using**

How This Helps Me

How This Hurts Me

_____   _____   _____

_____   _____   _____

_____   _____   _____

_____   _____   _____

_____   _____   _____

_____   _____   _____

_____   _____   _____

**Strategies I Will Need in
the Future**

How This Will Help Me Achieve My Goals

_____   _____

_____   _____

_____   _____

_____   _____

_____   _____

PERSONAL BEST

GOALS OF THE EXERCISE

1. Measure goal achievement in personal terms.
2. Break long-term goals into smaller achievable segments.
3. Affirm self for progress made toward long-term goals.
4. Recognize goal achievement as an ongoing process.

ADDITIONAL PROBLEMS FOR WHICH THIS EXERCISE MAY BE MOST USEFUL

- Attention-Deficit/Hyperactivity Disorder (ADHD)
- Learning Difficulties
- Oppositional Defiant Disorder (ODD)
- Responsible Behavior Training

SUGGESTIONS FOR USING THIS EXERCISE WITH STUDENT(S)

A personal best is an achievement signifying the student's best effort to date. Emphasizing personal best can help students with various talents and abilities to experience a sense of accomplishment as they work toward both short- and long-term academic, socioemotional, athletic, or personal goals. Each short-term goal reached becomes a new personal best accomplishment.

This exercise reinforces the idea that goal achievement should be measured in terms of personal progress, not by competing or comparing oneself with family members or other students. Ask the student to select a skill he or she would like to improve (e.g., cursive writing, math, technology competence, spelling, or a foreign language). Assist the student in determining a baseline level of performance (current level of functioning), a specific long-term goal, and a general short-term goal that can be used to identify and track progress (e.g., incrementally increasing legibility, speed, or, fluency; improving test scores; or increasing length of workouts or practice sessions).

Review the "Personal Best" activity with the student during each counseling session to ensure the student's up-to-date completion of the chart and graph, affirm the student for the progress made, and encourage the student's continued effort toward the long-term goal. This activity can be used to track progress toward goal achievement in several skill areas if student motivation and circumstances warrant.

PERSONAL BEST

Choose an activity or academic subject in which you would like to improve. Determine how you are going to measure your progress (e.g., grade, work sample, self-assessment, time on task, coach's rating). Before you begin to work, measure your performance on the subject or skill you have chosen to improve. This will be your baseline level of performance. If you are trying to improve your spelling scores, your baseline may be only two or three correct words on a quiz. If you are measuring your improvement in jumping rope, your baseline may be 5 or 10 jumps. As you study or practice, your skill will improve and you will achieve higher levels of performance. Each improved level that you measure is a personal best.

Record your improvement in scores, grades, or another method of assessment as you progress weekly or monthly throughout the year. Use the Personal Best Graph to record progress in one area of skill development. Shade in the graph and record the date of each personal best on the graph to measure both short- and long-term goal achievement.

Example

PERSONAL SKILL DEVELOPMENT

Subject/Activity	Unit of Measurement	Baseline/Date	Date and Improved Grade or Score
Cursive writing	*Handwriting samples*	*9/1: Name only*	*10/1: Writing whole alphabet and 25 words*
	Letter to parent		*12/1: 50 words*
	Class assignments		*3/1: 200 words*
			6/1: All assignments legible and in cursive

Short-Term Goal	Long-Term Goal	Percent of Progress Toward Goal
Increase speed and legibility	*All assignments legible and in cursive*	*10/1: 10%*
		12/1: 50%
		3/1: 75%
		6/1: 100%

PERSONAL BEST GRAPH

Tracking My Personal Progress

Shade or color in the graph and record the date as you progress toward your goal.

Example

Baseline:	Date:	Date:	Date:	Goal Achieved:
9/1	10/1	12/1	3/1	6/1

PERSONAL SKILL DEVELOPMENT

Subject/Activity	Unit of Measurement	Baseline/Date	Date and Improved Grade or Score
_____	_____	_____	_____
_____	_____	_____	_____
_____	_____	_____	_____
_____	_____	_____	_____
_____	_____	_____	_____
_____	_____	_____	_____
_____	_____	_____	_____
_____	_____	_____	_____

Short-Term Goal	Long-Term Goal	Percent of Progress Toward Goal
_____	_____	_____
_____	_____	_____

PERSONAL BEST GRAPH

Tracking My Personal Progress

Shade or color in the graph and record the date as you progress toward your goal.

Baseline:	Date:	Date:	Date:	Date:	Date:	Date:	Date:	Goal Achieved:
_____	_____	_____	_____	_____	_____	_____	_____	_____

CASES OF CONFLICT

GOALS OF THE EXERCISE

1. Recognize the roadblocks to effective anger management.
2. Practice effective strategies for a positive resolution to a conflict.
3. Identify the range of emotions experienced during a conflict.
4. Experience the effect of nonverbal communication on anger management.

ADDITIONAL PROBLEMS FOR WHICH THIS EXERCISE MAY BE MOST USEFUL

- Conflict Management
- Oppositional Defiant Disorder (ODD)
- Parenting Skills/Discipline
- Responsible Behavior Training
- Sibling Rivalry

SUGGESTIONS FOR USING THIS EXERCISE WITH STUDENT(S)

Most conflicts begin with a small triggering event and escalate because the disputants focus on their individual points of view and personal feelings rather than on working toward a mutually acceptable solution. The Cases of Conflict activity provides common power struggles or arguments that students experience in their daily lives. These examples of conflict can be used to study the anger, hurt, frustration, and resistance that occur during a conflict and to determine how verbal and nonverbal communication can contribute to either a peaceful or a highly antagonistic outcome.

Assign the student(s) to read one of the Cases of Conflict and role-play the situation to its conclusion by using negative nonverbal communication cues (e.g., rolling eyes, finger-pointing, raised eyebrows, folded arms) that contribute to increased anger and antagonism and a lose/lose outcome. Then have the student(s) role-play the same scenario by using positive nonverbal cues (e.g., smiling, eye contact, leaning toward the speaker, nodding the head) that contribute to a mutually agreeable win/win outcome.

Use the Cases of Conflict activity to teach additional strategies of anger management and conflict resolution, including brainstorming, effective listening, empathetic responses, "I" statements, and working for consensus. Act as an observer and stop the role-playing occasionally to increase awareness of the process, to point out specific techniques that are being used effectively or misused, and to guide the student(s) toward authentic consensual problem solving. This activity is appropriate for students in grades 3 to 12 and can be adapted for use with younger students.

CASES OF CONFLICT

SCENARIOS OF CONFLICT TO ROLE-PLAY, BRAINSTORM, AND RESOLVE

Read each scenario and make up an ending that might occur if the disputants use negative nonverbal communication cues (e.g., rolling eyes, finger-pointing, raised eyebrows, folded arms) that tend to increase the level of frustration and lack of cooperation. Then complete the same scenario by using positive nonverbal cues (e.g., smiling, eye contact, leaning toward the speaker, nodding the head) that contribute to a mutually agreeable solution. Role-play each outcome in your group or with your counselor.

Next use the Cases of Conflict to practice various responses to conflict. First, use negative approaches to resolve each conflict (e.g., arguing, fighting, sulking, walking away, using negative nonverbal cues) and role-play the outcome. Then, role-play positive methods to reach a mutually agreeable or win/win solution (e.g., listening, empathetic responses, brainstorming, using positive nonverbal cues, "I" statements).

1. **Playground Equipment**

    Jamaul and Arianna run outside when the recess bell rings. It is the first warm day of Spring and both have been waiting to jump-rope. The jump ropes are in a pile on the basketball court. Other students are looking for the jump ropes, too. By the time Jamaul and Arianna reach the pile, only one jump rope is left. Both grab for it, each holding on to one end. They face one another, each pulling on the rope. Jamaul looks at Arianna and says . . .

    Negative techniques that could be used: _____

    _____

    Negative outcome: _____

    _____

    Positive techniques that could be used: _____

    _____

    Positive outcome: _____

    _____

2. **Chores**

   Mother leaves a list of chores to be completed by the time she returns home from work on Saturday. She instructs Lyndsay and Sam to divide the chores evenly between them and make sure that the chores are finished before they get involved in any other activities. There are nine chores, so Lyndsay and Sam each take four. The remaining chore is to clean the upstairs bathroom. Each sibling thinks that this chore should be done by the other. They decide to resolve their difference of opinion by . . .

   Negative techniques that could be used: _____

   _____

   Negative outcome: _____

   _____

   Positive techniques that could be used: _____

   _____

   Positive outcome: _____

   _____

3. **First in Line**

   Rebecca and Martin bolt out of their seats when the teacher asks the class to line up for lunch. Martin pushes Rebecca and says, "I got here first." "Did not," Rebecca replies as she pushes him back. The teacher asks them to sit back down and decide how they are going to resolve the lining-up problem while she walks the rest of the class to lunch. She indicates that if they can't come up with a solution that will work for the rest of the year, she will think of something herself. Rebecca and Martin discuss the problem. They decide to . . .

   Negative techniques that could be used: _____

   _____

   Negative outcome: _____

   _____

   Positive techniques that could be used: _____

   _____

   Positive outcome: _____

   _____

4. **Road Rage**

   Jamie is late for school. He is driving fast because he doesn't want to get another tardy. Another car cuts him off just as he is about to pull into the fast lane and pass another car. He is furious and drives as close to the other car's bumper as possible while grimacing and gesturing with his hands. The other driver speeds up and gestures back to Jamie. Jamie stays right on his tail. Both cars pull into the school's parking lot. Jamie jumps out of his car and runs up to the other driver. He realizes it is another student from his Spanish class, who says, "Hey, man, you were following me real close." Jamie responds, ". . ."

   Negative techniques that could be used: _____

   _____

   Negative outcome: _____

   _____

   Positive techniques that could be used: _____

   _____

   Positive outcome: _____

   _____

5. **Remote Control**

   Destiny and Erika hit the family room couch at about the same time. They rarely agree on TV programs, and their new satellite dish makes choosing a program even more complicated. They both grab for the remote control, but Erika is the quickest and begins to channel-surf. Destiny walks up to the TV and stands in front of the screen. She says, "Erika, either we find something we both like or we won't be watching anything." Erika responds, "You always want your own way or nothing at all." At this point, their mother walks into the room, takes the remote control, and instructs the girls to work it out or lose their remote control privileges for one week. Destiny and Erika begin to . . .

   Negative techniques that could be used: _____

   _____

   Negative outcome: _____

   _____

   Positive techniques that could be used: _____

   _____

   Positive outcome: _____

   _____

6. **Competitive Games**

Anthony and Lamaar are playing a board game during indoor recess. Lamaar is winning, and when it is his turn, he takes a long time trying to decide on a strategy. Anthony is anxious to take his turn and try to regain the advantage. He becomes frustrated with Lamaar's slow play and gives him several looks, but Lamaar continues to take his time. Finally, Anthony decides to . . .

Negative techniques that could be used: _____

_____

Negative outcome: _____

_____

Positive techniques that could be used: _____

_____

Positive outcome: _____

_____

7. **Seats on the Bus**

Stephanie and Amilia plop into the same seat on the school bus. They wiggle and squirm, each trying to occupy the majority of the seat. They become so loud in their conquest that the bus driver gives them the evil eye in his rearview mirror. "Girls," he warns them, "decide who gets the seat or I will assign you seats for the rest of the semester." The girls react by . . .

Negative techniques that could be used: _____

_____

Negative outcome: _____

_____

Positive techniques that could be used: _____

_____

Positive outcome: _____

_____

8. **Put-Downs and Dissing**

Marquis and Carina arrive in their social skills class a few minutes early. Carina is wearing her favorite sweater, a Christmas present from her father. "Where'd you get that ugly sweater?" Marquis quips. "It's a whole lot better than anything I've seen you wearing," Carina replies with disgust. "Coming from you that's a compliment, since you have no taste," Marquis snaps back. Carina retorts, with fire in her eyes, "Just don't even talk to or look at me," to which Marquis replies nastily, "Your wish is my command, loser." At this point both students notice the teacher standing behind them, who says, "You know how I feel about dissing in general and especially

when you have come up with a plan for respecting one another's personal dignity."
The students move to the back of the room and begin to . . .

Negative techniques that could be used: _____

_____

Negative outcome: _____

_____

Positive techniques that could be used: _____

_____

Positive outcome: _____

_____

9. **Boyfriend/Girlfriend Disputes**

Brittany and Eric have been seeing each other since the beginning of the school year. Eric wants Brittany to go steady with him but insists that she first promise to spend more time with him and less time with her girlfriends. Brittany tells Eric that friendships are very important to her and accuses him of trying to control every part of her life. Eric says that Brittany's friends are jealous of him and are trying to break up their relationship. He insists that he really cares for Brittany but can't continue to see her if she insists on spending so much of her time with her girlfriends. Brittany wants to keep seeing Eric but has very uncomfortable feelings about agreeing to his terms for going steady. She decides to meet with him and . . .

Negative techniques that could be used: _____

_____

Negative outcome: _____

_____

Positive techniques that could be used: _____

_____

Positive outcome: _____

_____

Now work with your group to create a case of conflict to role-play by using both positive and negative techniques.

_____

_____

_____

_____

_____

_____

_____

Negative techniques that could be used: _____

_____

Negative outcome: _____

_____

Positive techniques that could be used: _____

_____

Positive outcome: _____

_____

COMMUNICATION WITH OTHERS

GOALS OF THE EXERCISE

1. Recognize that communication involves both listening and speaking.
2. Develop assertive strategies for self-expression.
3. Define appropriate times for listening.
4. Define appropriate times for speaking.

ADDITIONAL PROBLEMS FOR WHICH THIS EXERCISE MAY BE MOST USEFUL

- Attention-Seeking Behavior
- Conflict Management
- Depression
- Self-Esteem Building
- Social Skills/Peer Relationships

SUGGESTIONS FOR USING THIS EXERCISE WITH STUDENT(S)

Students often view communication with others as self-expression or talking to others. This activity is designed to teach both aspects of communication: speaking and listening. Discuss with the student, either individually or in a group session, that there are appropriate times to speak and appropriate times to listen. Give some examples of each. Appropriate times to listen might be during teacher instruction, at church, and while a friend is talking; appropriate times to speak might be during class discussion, while giving directions, and while communicating an idea, thought, or feeling. Brainstorm with the student(s) additional ideas for listening and speaking and record the ideas in the spaces provided on the worksheet. After all of the spaces are filled in with appropri-ate responses, assign the student(s) to draw a picture or write a short story of a good time for him or her to listen and a good time for him or her to express ideas, thoughts, or feelings. This activity is appropriate for students in grades kindergarten through 5.

COMMUNICATION WITH OTHERS

Communication involves both speaking and listening and knowing the appropriate time for each. Think of some times when it's important to listen and some other times when it's important to speak up and express yourself. Consider situations at home, school, and during other activities when you use these communication skills. After you have written your ideas, draw a picture of yourself communicating by listening and another of yourself speaking up.

Appropriate Times for Listening

_____

_____

_____

_____

A good time to listen (picture or story):

Appropriate Times for Speaking

_____

_____

_____

_____

A good time to speak up (picture or story):

MISTAKE OR LEARNING OPPORTUNITY?

GOALS OF THE EXERCISE

1. Recognize that mistakes are an essential part of learning.
2. Record the lesson learned from several personal mistakes.
3. Identify a positive change in behavior resulting from a mistake.
4. Reduce feelings of guilt and frustration linked to personal mistakes.
5. Verbalize the knowledge that all people make mistakes.

ADDITIONAL PROBLEMS FOR WHICH THIS EXERCISE MAY BE MOST USEFUL

- Anger Management/Aggression
- Attention-Deficit/Hyperactivity Disorder (ADHD)
- Attention-Seeking Behavior
- Conflict Management

SUGGESTIONS FOR USING THIS EXERCISE WITH STUDENT(S)

Generally, students try to avoid making mistakes, but when they make them, they try to cover them up and feel frustrated, angry, embarrassed, and guilty as a result. Ideally, students should be taught from early childhood that mistakes are a natural part of learning that can strengthen and enrich life. This activity can help the student differentiate chronic mistakes that he or she has repeated with no lesson learned and no change in behavior (unproductive mistakes) from mistakes that teach him or her important lessons and change future behavior (productive mistakes).

Ask the student to read the introduction to the activity and discuss the meaning of a learning opportunity (e.g., a chance to learn a lesson that will improve personal coping skills). Read and discuss the examples provided with the student and ask the student to record several mistakes he or she can recall making. If the student is in early elementary school, assist in recording his or her ideas. Take time to explore the lessons learned and the future benefits of each mistake. Students may enjoy and gain additional insight by drawing a picture of a mistake made and a follow-up picture of the lesson they have learned, as well as describing what they plan to do next time if they find themselves in a similar situation. Drawings can be done by using the sequential cartoon frames provided in the activity. The student who maintains a personal or counseling journal should keep this activity in that folder. The activity may take several sessions to complete, depending on the amount of dialogue and pictures that are elicited. Brainstorm the most difficult aspects first, followed by the benefits of making a mistake; then ask the student to record his or her favorite ideas in the space provided at the bottom of the activity sheet. This activity is appropriate for students in grades 4 through 12 and can be adapted for use with younger students.

MISTAKE OR LEARNING OPPORTUNITY?

Mistakes are things we usually try to avoid. However, if mistakes are looked at as learning opportunities rather than something that shouldn't happen to us, they can help us develop problem-solving skills and better ways of handling the many challenges in our lives. List several personal mistakes in the column on the left. Then list the lesson that could be learned from that mistake and the future benefits that can be gained from the experience.

Mistake	**Lesson Learned**	**Future Benefits**
Examples:		
I left my baseball glove out in the yard.	*Rain can ruin a good baseball glove.*	*I'll take better care of my important belongings.*
I ran out of gas on the way to school.	*It's a big hassle to run out of gas.*	*I'll get gas when the gas needle reads low.*
I didn't study for a test.	*Failure to study causes poor grades.*	*I'll study so I can succeed in school.*

1. _____ _____ _____

2. _____ _____ _____

3. _____ _____ _____

4. _____ _____ _____

5. _____ _____ _____

6. _____ _____ _____

7. _____ _____ _____

8. _____ _____ _____

9. _____ _____ _____

10. _____ _____ _____

11. _____ _____ _____

12. _____   _____   _____

13. _____   _____   _____

14. _____   _____   _____

15. _____   _____   _____

The hardest part of making a mistake is _____
_____

The benefits of making a mistake are _____
_____

When a mistake helps you learn a better way to handle a problem or challenge, it is called a productive mistake. Draw a picture or cartoon about a mistake that helped you learn an important lesson.

A mistake I once made:

```



```

The lesson I learned:

```



```

Next time I face the same situation, I will:

```



```

PHYSICAL RECEPTORS OF STRESS

GOALS OF THE EXERCISE

1. Identify how stress is demonstrated in physical symptoms.
2. Recognize the positive and the negative aspects of stress.
3. Differentiate between long- and short-term stress.
4. Implement techniques to counter the negative aspects of chronic stress.

ADDITIONAL PROBLEMS FOR WHICH THIS EXERCISE MAY BE MOST USEFUL

- Anger Management/Aggression
- Attention-Deficit/Hyperactivity Disorder (ADHD)
- Depression
- Divorce
- Grief/Loss
- Responsible Behavior Training

SUGGESTIONS FOR USING THIS EXERCISE WITH STUDENT(S)

The Physical Receptors of Stress activity helps the student pinpoint the areas of his or her body that harbor anxiety and stress. Review with the student the short- and long-term results of stress, which are listed on the Physical Receptors of Stress activity sheet. Point out that the short-term results of stress can be helpful and positive as they heighten the ability of the body and mind to address a threat or problem. However, the long-term effects of chronic stress are physically, mentally, socially, and emotionally harmful.

Instruct the student to identify physical areas where personal stress is evident and mark them with a colored pencil or marker on a full-body drawing or photo of him- or herself that he or she draws or pastes on the activity sheet. Discuss how stress manifests itself in these physical receptors. Instruct the student to be alert to stress in his or her body between counseling sessions and to identify and mark on the human figure new and recurring physical receptors as they are recognized, using a pencil or marker of a different color. Review the identified physical receptors with the student during the next counseling session. This activity is appropriate for students in grades 5 through 12.

INSTRUCTIONS FOR THE STUDENT

Stress is created by your body's natural reaction to a perceived threat or problem and the resulting fight-or-flight response intended originally for self-protection. Your stress reactors were designed to deal with a problem within a short period and then return to a more normal, relaxed state. Chronic or constant stress keeps the body's alert systems active over long periods. This causes both physical and mental damage as a result of the toxic chemicals (adrenaline and cortisol) that remain in the system, rather than being released from the body as nature had intended. Constant stress can lead to fatigue, anger, depression, diminished cognitive ability, suppression of the immune system, and many other physical problems. Symptoms of chronic stress can often be harbored in particular parts of the body and are indicated by tightness, stiffness, weakness, and/or pain (e.g., a tight jaw; a headache; shoulder, neck, or lower back pain; a stomachache; chest pains).

Keep track of where stress affects your body most often. Use a pencil or colored marker to pinpoint the areas where you feel stress during the following week. Each time you feel stress in your body, record the location on the picture or photo of yourself. This process will help you identify how your body reacts to challenging situations.

Some antidotes for the physical symptoms of stress include listening to music or relaxation tapes, aerobic exercise, sequential muscle relaxation, rhythmic breathing, humor, and talking with a friend. Talk with your counselor about how these antidotes can help you deal with challenges without becoming overly stressed or developing physical symptoms. Choose one of the antidotes and practice it between counseling sessions. Report the results of your stress-fighting program during your next counseling session.

PHYSICAL RECEPTORS OF STRESS

LONG- AND SHORT-TERM PHYSICAL EFFECTS OF STRESS

Paste a photo or draw an outline of a human figure similar to yourself in the center box. Record the most common areas where you feel stress in your body during the following week.

Short-term stress makes us more mentally and physically alert and able to deal with the problem.	Long-term or chronic stress threatens our physical and mental health.
Short-term results: The body prepares to deal with the problem.	Long term results: The body is unable to release harmful chemicals designed to cope with short-term stress.

- **Brain:** Improved thinking and reduced sense of pain
- **Eyes:** Improved vision
- **Lungs:** Increased oxygen intake
- **Heart:** Increased heart rate and blood pressure
- **Adrenal glands:** Adrenaline released into body
- **Intestines:** Digestion stops to allow for increased energy in muscles
- **Hair:** Body hair stands up

- **Brain:** Released cortisol becomes harmful to brain cells Fatigue, anger, and depression result
- **Immune system:** Weakened resistance to disease
- **Intestines:** Reduction of blood flow increases chance of ulcers
- **Circulation:** Higher blood pressure and heart rate; damaged blood vessels

101 WAYS TO COPE WITH STRESS

GOALS OF THE EXERCISE

1. Recognize the availability of many strategies to cope with anxiety.
2. Verbalize confidence in the ability to reduce personal anxiety.
3. Implement coping strategies to reduce symptoms of stress.
4. Recognize personal behavior that contributes to stress.

ADDITIONAL PROBLEMS FOR WHICH THIS EXERCISE MAY BE MOST USEFUL

- Anger Management/Aggression
- Attention-Deficit/Hyperactivity Disorder (ADHD)
- Substance Abuse
- Suicide Ideation Attempt

SUGGESTIONS FOR USING THIS EXERCISE WITH STUDENT(S)

The 101 Ways to Cope with Stress activity can be used to help students evaluate stress and anxiety from several different perspectives. An elevated level of anxiety is often coupled with the perception that no viable solution for stress reduction exists. This list offers the student numerous options for reducing anxiety.

Read the entire list with the student. Ask him or her to circle any strategies he or she has tried and found useful. Stop to discuss or explain any strategies that are unclear to the student or perceived as unworkable.

Ask the student if any of the coping strategies suggest behavior that is counterproductive to stress-busting (e.g., number 37 of the list might suggest that taking life too seriously contributes to anxiety; number 4 might suggest that substance abuse is counterproductive). Instruct the student to highlight all strategies that point to a personal behavior contributing to his or her stress level.

Discuss with the student how different coping strategies from the list might alter his or her level of stress or anxiety. Ask him or her to pick two or three that might work to reduce the level of stress and choose one to implement between counseling sessions. Explore with the student the specifics of how and when to use the strategy and brainstorm its potential results. Review the outcome at the next session and elicit an agreement to either continue with the strategy or choose another from the list.

INSTRUCTIONS FOR THE STUDENT

Read over the 101 Ways to Cope with Stress list and circle all of the strategies that you already use to cope with stress. Ask for an explanation of any of the ideas that are unclear or that you think may not work to reduce your level of stress. Determine which strategies are most helpful to you, and choose one or two to use more frequently as stress reducers during the following week. Discuss with your counselor or group members why you have chosen these particular actions to reduce your level of stress.

During the next counseling session, report to your counselor or group how the interventions you picked affected your level of stress during the week. Choose two additional strategies that you want to add to your stress reduction program. Continue to try different strategies during the weeks ahead, and review the effects of each action during your next counseling session.

After several weeks of trying different methods of reducing your personal level of stress and anxiety, create your own top 10 list of effective stress reducers. Write this list in a personal journal and review and modify it occasionally throughout the year.

101 WAYS TO COPE WITH STRESS

1. Get up earlier
2. Prepare ahead
3. Avoid tight clothes
4. Avoid chemical aids
5. Set appointments
6. Write it down
7. Practice preventive maintenance
8. Make duplicate keys
9. Say "no" more often
10. Set priorities
11. Avoid negative people
12. Use time wisely
13. Simplify meals
14. Copy important papers
15. Anticipate needs
16. Make repairs
17. Get help with jobs you dislike
18. Break down large tasks
19. Look at problems as challenges
20. Look at challenges differently
21. Unclutter your life
22. Smile
23. Prepare for rain
24. Tickle a baby
25. Pet a dog or cat

26. Don't know all the answers
27. Look for the silver lining
28. Say something nice
29. Teach a kid to fly a kite
30. Walk in the rain
31. Schedule playtime
32. Take a bubble bath
33. Be aware of your decisions
34. Believe in yourself
35. Stop talking negatively
36. Visualize winning
37. Develop a sense of humor
38. Stop thinking tomorrow will be better
39. Have goals
40. Dance a jig
41. Say hello to a stranger
42. Ask a friend for a hug
43. Look at the stars
44. Breathe slowly
45. Whistle a tune
46. Read a poem
47. Listen to a symphony
48. Watch a ballet
49. Read a story

50. Do something new
51. Stop a bad habit
52. Buy a flower
53. Smell a flower
54. Find support
55. Find a "venting partner"
56. Do it today
57. Be optimistic
58. Put safety first
59. Do things in moderation
60. Note your appearance
61. Strive for excellence, not perfection
62. Stretch your limits
63. Enjoy art
64. Hum a jingle
65. Maintain your weight
66. Plant a tree
67. Feed the birds
68. Practice grace
69. Stretch
70. Have a plan B
71. Doodle
72. Learn a joke
73. Know your feelings
74. Meet your needs
75. Know your limits
76. Say "Have a good day" in pig Latin
77. Throw a paper airplane
78. Exercise
79. Learn a new song
80. Go to work earlier
81. Clean a closet
82. Play with a child
83. Go on a picnic
84. Drive a different route to work
85. Leave work early
86. Put air freshener in your car
87. Watch a movie and eat popcorn
88. Write a faraway friend
89. Scream at a ball game
90. Eat a meal by candlelight
91. Recognize the importance of unconditional love
92. Remember that stress is an attitude
93. Keep a journal
94. Share a monster smile
95. Remember your options
96. Build a support network
97. Quit trying to fix others
98. Get enough sleep
99. Talk less and listen more
100. Praise others
101. Relax, take each day one at a time . . . you have the rest of your life to live

(Information provided with permission from Kids-in-Touch, a division of West Michigan Addiction Consultants, PC. Phone: 616-365-8800; website: alcoholism.about.com)

STUDENT AND FAMILY HISTORY FORM

GOALS OF THE EXERCISE

1. Parents provide background information and developmental history to the assessment team.
2. Parents consider issues that may affect or influence the student's adjustment and progress in school.
3. Parents become members of the student assessment team.
4. Facilitate and enhance communication between parents and the student assessment team.

ADDITIONAL PROBLEMS FOR WHICH THIS EXERCISE MAY BE MOST USEFUL

- Attention-Deficit/Hyperactivity Disorder (ADHD)
- Depression
- Learning Difficulties
- Oppositional Defiant Disorder (ODD)
- Physical Disabilities/Challenges
- Social Maladjustment/Conduct Disorder

SUGGESTIONS FOR USING THIS EXERCISE WITH STUDENT(S)

Parents are an essential part of the school's multidisciplinary evaluation team, and their unique and intimate knowledge of the student is key to the assessment process for determining eligibility for special education, 504 accommodations, or additional regular education services. The Student and Family History Form guides the parents to consider their child and his or her adjustment and current functioning from several perspectives. The parent is asked to provide information about the student's background, medical history, personal characteristics, interests, strengths, and weaknesses. The form is comprehensive, organized, and somewhat lengthy. Parents are asked to complete the form before meeting with a member of the student assessment team. Completing the form will help them to formulate their thoughts and concerns in preparation for the interview session and assist them in their role as student advocate at the individualized education planning and placement committee (IEPC) and other meetings with school staff. The parents' time and emotional energy spent completing the form contribute greatly to the quality of the assessment; their cooperation should be encouraged and acknowledged.

INSTRUCTIONS FOR USING THE STUDENT AND FAMILY HISTORY FORM

Give or send the Student and Family History Form to the parent(s) after an initial meeting or phone call to communicate the school's concern and explain the proposed evaluation or assessment process. Ask the parent(s) to complete the form in as much detail as possible and to return it before the formal parent input interview. A school-addressed stamped envelope will facilitate the return of the form in many cases. Advise the parent(s) to phone for clarification if any part of the form is confusing or if there is information they can't remember or don't have access to. Encourage the parent(s) to obtain medical or therapeutic records or any additional information that is relevant to the student's presenting difficulties and that would help the assessment team complete the evaluation and determine appropriate services.

STUDENT AND FAMILY HISTORY FORM

Dear Parent,

In order to conduct a comprehensive evaluation of your child's social, emotional, and academic adjustment in school, your input is a necessary component. All information you provide will be kept confidential and will be used in determining eligibility for special services or accommodations that may be effective in enhancing your child's performance in the school setting. Please complete and return this form to me at your earliest convenience. If you have any questions concerning this form or the evaluation process, please call me at _____.

Sincerely,
Title: _____
School: _____
Address: _____

Student's Name: _____ Date: _____

Form completed by: _____ Relationship to student: _____

How would you describe your child's adjustment to school?

_____

_____

_____

_____

_____

What is your child's greatest difficulty in school?

_____

_____

_____

_____

_____

_____

List five strengths and five weaknesses you observe in your child:

Strengths	**Weaknesses**
1. _____	1. _____
2. _____	2. _____
3. _____	3. _____
4. _____	4. _____
5. _____	5. _____

How would you describe your child's behavior at home (e.g., cooperation, self-discipline, responsible behavior, trustworthiness, following rules)?

_____

_____

_____

_____

How does your child relate to

Family members: _____

Siblings: _____

Friends or peers: _____

Teachers or mentors: _____

Did your child experience any problems at birth or during the first year (e.g., eating, sleeping, snuggling, smiling, eye contact, or other health concerns)?

_____

_____

_____

_____

Are there current health factors that may be affecting your child's school performance (e.g., vision, hearing, allergies, seizures)?

_____

_____

_____

_____

Are there socioemotional, family, or other factors now or in the past that may be contributing to your child's school performance?

_____

_____

_____

_____

How would you describe your child's ability to speak and use language?

_____

_____

_____

_____

What suggestions do you have for helping your child to become more successful in school?

_____

_____

_____

_____

What are your child's leisure-time activities?

_____

_____

What is your child's bedtime?

_____

Additional comments:

_____

_____

_____

_____

_____

DEVELOPMENTAL HISTORY

Student's name: _____ Date of birth: _____ Age: _____

Father's name: _____ Age: _____

Mother's name: _____ Age: _____

PREGNANCY AND BIRTH

Pregnancy: Planned or unplanned: _____

Length of pregnancy: Full term? _____ Premature (what month)? _____

Illnesses during pregnancy: _____
_____

Delivery (e.g., easy, difficult, normal, breach, instruments used, hours of labor):
_____
_____

Birthweight: _____ lbs. _____ oz. Length at birth: _____

Other comments about the pregnancy or birth: _____
_____
_____

Problems the child or mother had immediately after birth: _____
_____
_____

Place of birth (hospital or home): _____ City: _____

Attending physician(s): _____

Mother's age at time of delivery: _____

Total number of pregnancies of the mother: _____

The student is the _____ (birth order among siblings) of _____ (total number) siblings.

Problems that the student's siblings had during pregnancy or birth: _____

_____

Is the child adopted? _____

Age of adoption and circumstances if adopted: _____

_____

_____

EARLY INFANCY (BIRTH TO ONE YEAR)

Please check items that characterize your child:

_____	Breast-fed to age _____	_____	Resisted solid foods
_____	Bottle-fed to age _____	_____	Frequent rocking or banging of head
_____	Colicky	_____	Too active
_____	Eczema	_____	Did not like to be held
_____	Cuddly	_____	Rarely cried
_____	Difficult to feed	_____	Difficulty gaining weight

Additional comments about your child during early infancy:

_____

_____

DEVELOPMENTAL STAGES

Indicate the age when the following developmental milestones took place:

_____	First smiled	_____	Weaned from bottle or breast
_____	Sat up alone	_____	Toilet training began
_____	Crawled	_____	Day wetting ended
_____	Stood alone	_____	Night wetting ended
_____	Walked independently	_____	Bowel soiling ended

Additional comments:

_____

_____

Describe your child now (check where appropriate):

_____	Absentminded	_____	Easily frightened
_____	Affectionate	_____	Eating difficulties
_____	Considerate	_____	Friendly
_____	Cries excessively	_____	Happy
_____	Dependable	_____	Irritable
_____	Destructive	_____	Keeps feelings to self
_____	Difficulties with parents	_____	Lonely
_____	Difficulties with siblings	_____	Moody
_____	Difficulties with teachers	_____	Nightmares
_____	Obedient	_____	Shy
_____	Overactive	_____	Steals
_____	Restless sleeper	_____	Temper tantrums
_____	Self-reliant	_____	Underactive
_____	Sensitive	_____	Unduly dependent
_____	Serious	_____	Wanders or runs away from home

Fears (please list): _____

Learning difficulties (e.g., reading, speech): _____

_____

Special interests or hobbies: _____

_____

_____

Additional comments about your child's current characteristics or behavior:

_____

_____

MEDICAL INFORMATION

Please check any medical conditions that apply to your child:

_____	Allergies	_____	Heart disease
_____	Asthma	_____	Hernia
_____	Chicken pox	_____	High fevers
_____	Convulsions	_____	Overweight
_____	Deliriums	_____	Paralysis
_____	Ear infections	_____	Pneumonia
_____	Eczema	_____	Rheumatic fever
_____	Fainting spells	_____	Tonsillitis
_____	Food sensitivities	_____	Underweight
_____	Frequent colds		

Accidents, surgeries, or hospitalizations (please describe):

_____   Age _____
_____   Age _____
_____   Age _____
_____   Age _____

Therapy (physical or psychological):

_____   Age _____   Length _____
_____   Age _____   Length _____
_____   Age _____   Length _____

Is your child taking any type of prescribed or over-the-counter medication? Please list type and prescribing doctor: _____

_____

Has your child had a hearing test?   Date _____   Results _____
Has your child had a vision test?   Date _____   Results _____

SCHOOL INFORMATION

Has your child ever had difficulties in school (please describe)?

_____

_____

_____

When did these difficulties begin (e.g., age, grade, time of year)?

_____

What appeared to trigger these difficulties?

_____

_____

_____

How old was the student when he or she began school? _____

Please list all of your child's school experiences, including preschool, kindergarten, tutoring, summer school, accelerated classes, and special education.

Experience _____   Age _____
Experience _____   Age _____
Experience _____   Age _____
Experience _____   Age _____
Experience _____   Age _____

Last grade completed: _____

Current school attending or enrolled for next semester: _____

Signature: _____

Date: _____

STUDENT INTERVIEW OUTLINE

GOALS OF THE EXERCISE

1. Develop a positive relationship and establish a level of trust with the therapist.
2. Actively participate in the assessment process.
3. Share background information and feelings about school and personal life.
4. Identify factors contributing to the presenting problem.

ADDITIONAL PROBLEMS FOR WHICH THIS EXERCISE MAY BE MOST USEFUL

- Attention-Deficit/Hyperactivity Disorder (ADHD)
- Depression
- Learning Difficulties
- Oppositional Defiant Disorder (ODD)
- Physical Disabilities/Challenges
- Social Maladjustment/Conduct Disorder

SUGGESTIONS FOR USING THIS EXERCISE WITH STUDENT(S)

The Student Interview Outline provides the school mental health specialist (e.g., school counselor, social worker, psychologist) with a structured guideline for gathering essential data from the student's perspective. The outline is designed to be used with students of all ages, from early childhood through young adulthood, with only minor changes in wording left to the interviewer's discretion.

During this structured interview, the interviewer is able to assess the student's speech and language skills; knowledge of concrete personal data; ability to imagine and think abstractly; ability to test reality; attitude toward school; level of self-esteem; ability to solve problems; expression of personal feelings and defensiveness; family relationships; plans for the future; and awareness of personal problems, including the presenting problem. The interview questions allow a positive relationship between student and interviewer to develop in a low-key, nonthreatening manner. The questions begin very simply and gradually increase in intensity only after trust has been established. Completion of the outline may take up to three sessions or two to three hours, depending on the student's willingness to share and the length of his or her verbalizations.

INSTRUCTIONS FOR ADMINISTERING THE STUDENT INTERVIEW OUTLINE

Before the interview, explain to the student that his or her teacher or parent has asked you to meet with him or her. Ask some questions about home, school, and favorite activities. Indicate that you are trying to find out if there is anything the school or family can do to help him or her become more successful in school. Share any additional referral information that may be useful in encouraging the student to cooperate with the interview. Tell the student that he or she is a key important factor in the assessment process for gathering information and determining solutions for success. Ask the student if he or she has any questions; then begin the structured interview.

The outline begins with concrete questions about the student's personal data (e.g., name, address) and family and school background; then it moves to a more abstract exploration of thoughts, feelings, dreams, reality testing, and positive and negative experiences. The student is asked to assess personal strengths and weaknesses, future plans, and desired changes in him- or herself and family members. Finally, the presenting problem is explored, and the student's input regarding possible solutions is requested.

STUDENT INTERVIEW OUTLINE

I. PERSONAL DATA

How do you spell your first name? _____

How do you spell your last name? _____

What is your middle name? _____

Do you have any nicknames? _____

What do you like to be called best? _____

What is your address? _____

When is your birthday? month: _____ day: _____ year: _____

What is your age? _____

II. FAMILY INFORMATION

What is your father's name? _____ age: _____

Father's address: _____

Occupation: _____

Who does your father live with? _____

_____

What is your mother's name? _____ age: _____

Mother's address: _____

Occupation: _____

Who does your mother live with? _____

_____

Do you have any brother or sisters? _____ How many? _____

First and last name of sibling:	Age:	School and grade:	Living with:
_____	____	_____	_____
_____	____	_____	_____
_____	____	_____	_____
_____	____	_____	_____
_____	____	_____	_____

III. SCHOOL INFORMATION

What is the name of your school? _____

What grade are you in? _____   Teacher's name: _____

What subjects or activities do you do well in? _____

_____

What subjects or activities do you struggle with? _____

_____

Why are these subjects or activities difficult for you? _____

_____

What is your favorite thing about school? _____

_____

Are there some things you dislike about school? _____

_____

What was your best year or class in school? _____

Why? _____

What was your worst year or class in school? _____

Why? _____

IV. HOBBIES AND INTERESTS

What do you do after school? _____

_____

What is your favorite way to spend time? _____

_____

Name several of your hobbies or interests. _____

_____

What kinds of books do you like? _____

_____

What movies or videos have you seen that you like? _____

_____

Do you belong to any clubs, teams, or church or other activity groups? _____

_____

V. FACTS, FANTASY, AND WISHES

If you could choose, how old would you like to be?

Older: _____   Younger: _____   Same age: _____

Why? _____

_____

Tell me three things that are true:

_____

_____

_____

Tell me three things that are impossible (not true):

_____

_____

_____

Tell me about a dream you have had, or make up a short story:

_____

_____

_____

_____

What is the first thing you can remember in your life? How old were you? _____

_____

_____

_____

_____

What is the best thing that has ever happened to you?

_____

_____

_____

What is the worst thing that has ever happened to you?

_____

_____

_____

Who do you admire most? _____
Why? _____

Is there anyone you strongly dislike or despise? _____
Why? _____

VI. PERSONAL ASSESSMENT

List your personal strengths and assets and the things you like about yourself:

_____

_____

_____

List your personal weaknesses and the things you dislike about yourself:

_____

_____

_____

Have you ever felt that you would like to change places with someone? Explain.

_____

_____

_____

When you grow up and leave school, what would you like to do? Why?

_____

_____

_____

Suppose you could change all or part of someone's personal characteristics or behavior. How would you change yourself?

_____

_____

_____

How would you change your father?

_____

_____

_____

How would you change your mother?

_____

_____

_____

Is there anyone else in your family you would like to change?

_____

_____

_____

VII. PERSONAL FEELINGS

Everyone gets angry or mad sometimes. When do you get angry or lose your temper?

_____

_____

What do you do when you get angry (e.g., How do you look, feel, and act)?

_____

_____

When do you get angry at your mother?

_____

_____

When do you get angry at your father?

_____

_____

When do you get angry at your siblings?

_____

_____

When do you get angry at your teacher?

_____

_____

When do you get angry at your classmates or friends?

_____

_____

When do other people become angry with you?

_____

_____

Have you ever wanted to seek revenge or get even with someone? Explain.

_____

_____

When do you feel unhappy or sad?

_____

_____

When do you feel like crying?

_____

_____

When do you feel sorry for something you have done?

_____

_____

How do you apologize or make things up to someone you have hurt?

_____

_____

What kinds of things do you worry about?

_____

_____

VIII. ADDRESSING THE PRESENTING PROBLEM

What is the problem that you or others who know you are most concerned about (e.g., the presenting or identified problem)?

_____

_____

Do you know why you are working with me today?

_____

_____

Is anyone else helping you to resolve this problem? Explain.

_____

_____

What can you do to resolve this problem?

_____

_____

What can others do to help you resolve this problem?

_____

_____

GROWING AND CHANGING

GOALS OF THE EXERCISE

1. Recognize that learning, changing, and self-improvement is a lifelong process.
2. Affirm self for skills and abilities that you have mastered.
3. Identify positive learning goals for the future.
4. Recognize school as an essential component of becoming a competent, successful adult.

ADDITIONAL PROBLEMS IN WHICH THIS EXERCISE MAY BE USEFUL

- Depression
- Blended Family
- Attention-Seeking Behavior
- Learning Difficulties

SUGGESTIONS FOR PROCESSING THIS EXERCISE WITH STUDENT(S)

Many students view learning and skill development as a time-limited process. It is not unusual to hear a first-grader say that he or she has *learned* to read rather than he or she is *learning* to read. This activity will help the student view learning, growing, changing, and reaching his or her future goals as a lifelong process that began at birth and will continue indefinitely. The activity asks the student to remember significant developmental milestones that occurred when he or she was a baby, when beginning school, and when he or she progressed through the grades. The student is then prompted to record important learning that will take place in future grades and as an adult.

Encourage the student to affirm him- or herself for learning, skill development, and particularly for socioemotional growth that has already taken place. This will help the student look to the future with optimism and with motivation for becoming a stronger, more capable individual. This activity can be used with students of all ages to develop their ability to set goals for the future growth and to see themselves as a work in progress.

GROWING AND CHANGING

You have been growing and changing since well before you were born. During the first year of your life you changed from a very small and helpless baby to a toddler who could make his or her wishes known and communicate with a highly effective combination of sounds, expressions, and gestures. Since that first year you have grown even stronger and more capable each day. Each person develops skills and abilities at their own pace, but everyone becomes a little more able to manage his or her life and better prepared for future independence as he or she grows and changes.

List several of the important things you have learned so far in your life. If you have trouble remembering the things you learned as a baby or a kindergartner, ask a parent or another adult who knew you then. Try to imagine what your life was like when you didn't have all of the skills and abilities you have now.

If you are in middle school or high school, list the things that you are learning that will influence your life in the future. If not, try to think of the many lessons you will learn during your secondary school years. Include academic, career preparation, athletic, social, emotional, musical, artistic, and other areas that will be important to helping you become the adult you want to be.

Finally, consider yourself as an adult. What will you be learning about then? Remember that learning is an ongoing process that hopefully will continue throughout your lifetime. When you have finished the Growing and Changing activity, find some photographs that show you learning something significant as a baby or toddler, as a preschooler or kindergartner, as an elementary school student, and as a secondary school (junior high or high school) student. If you don't have pictures of yourself, draw one of yourself growing and changing in significant ways. Share your ideas and pictures with your parents, teachers, and the social worker or counselor who assigned this activity to you.

GROWING AND CHANGING

Each Day, I Become Stronger and More Capable

When I was a baby and toddler, I learned how to:

_____   _____

_____   _____

_____   _____

In preschool and kindergarten, I learned how to:

_____   _____

_____   _____

_____   _____

During elementary school, I learned how to:

_____   _____

_____   _____

_____   _____

In middle and high school, I will learn or have learned how to:

_____   _____

_____   _____

_____   _____

As an adult, I will learn how to:

_____   _____

_____   _____

_____   _____

Draw or paste a picture of yourself learning something as a baby or toddler.

Draw or paste a picture of yourself learning something as a preschooler or kindergartner.

Draw or paste a picture of yourself learning something in elementary school.

Draw or paste a picture of yourself learning something in middle school or high school.

Draw a picture of yourself learning something as an adult.

MY PREDICTIONS FOR THE FUTURE

GOALS OF THE EXERCISE

1. Establish positive goals for the future.
2. Plan for future family needs and employment.
3. Relate current behavior to future goals.
4. Consider lifelong learning and problem-solving skills as essential for future prosperity.

ADDITIONAL PROBLEMS FOR WHICH THIS EXERCISE MAY BE MOST USEFUL

*   Career Planning
*   Learning Difficulties
*   Responsible Behavior Training
*   Self-Esteem Building

SUGGESTIONS FOR USING THIS EXERCISE WITH STUDENT(S)

My Predictions for the Future will help the student begin to picture his or her life as an adult and consider which issues will be most important to him or her at that time. Issues of family, work, continuing education, problem solving, and leisure time are addressed by using sentence starters that the student is asked to complete. Students are often quite shortsighted in terms of planning for their futures. Self-defeating or resistant behavior is often directed at solving immediate or short-term problems rather than considering how current experiences can affect future well-being.

When the student has completed the activity, the responses should be reviewed in a counseling session to guide his or her thinking toward preparing for future happiness, self-sufficiency, and prosperity. The student can then begin to consider which current behaviors and perceptions are contributing to a satisfying future and which are not. This activity is appropriate for students in grades 4 through 12.

MY PREDICTIONS FOR THE FUTURE

Planning and predicting how your life will be in the future helps you begin to prepare now, during your school years. It is important to have a dream or goal for how you will live, learn, work, and enjoy your leisure time in the future. Will you live in a family, with friends, or by yourself? What type of work will you do? Will you continue to learn and experience new things? What issues will be the most important to you? Start thinking about your future now by completing the following sentences. This will help you begin moving toward a satisfying, meaningful life as an adult. When you have completed the predictions, add to your ideas and draw a picture of yourself in the future.

As an adult I will become _____

I will live _____
with _____

My leisure (fun) activities will include _____
_____

I will want to learn more about _____
and will further my education by _____

I will stay healthy because I will _____
_____

My friends will be _____
_____

My life will be much different because _____
_____

The most difficult thing about my life will be _____
_____

But because I will be a good problem solver, I will _____

_____

The most important thing to me will be _____

_____

_____

_____

Add to your predictions if you wish.

_____

_____

_____

_____

_____

_____

Draw a picture of yourself in the future:

SUMMARY OF ADHD ASSESSMENTS

GOALS OF THE EXERCISE

1. Assess the student for symptoms of ADHD using various scales, indexes, observations, personal records, and interviews.
2. Record the results of the ADHD assessments and related information using one document.
3. Report the results of the ADHD assessments to the student's parents and doctor.
4. Compare the results of the assessments completed by the student's parents with those completed by the school.

ADDITIONAL PROBLEMS FOR WHICH THIS EXERCISE MAY BE MOST USEFUL

- Academic Motivation
- Oppositional Defiant Disorder (ODD)
- Assessment for Special Services
- Learning Difficulties

SUGGESTIONS FOR USING THIS EXERCISE WITH STUDENT(S)

The decision to use medication to treat ADHD requires serious consideration by the student's doctor and parents as well as the student. A thorough assessment of the student's symptoms and current functioning is essential. Numerous scales and indexes are available for use by teachers and parents to evaluate the student's current functioning for possible indications of ADHD. The Summary of ADHD Assessments allows the school social worker, counselor, or psychologist to organize the results of various assessment scales, informal interviews, and observations using one document. This form can then be used to submit assessment results to the student's doctor and to inform the parents of the results and indications of the assessment.

The Summary of ADHD Assessments creates a record of past and ongoing assessments, and it documents the evaluation work done by the school. A copy of the assessment summary should be placed in the student's cumulative record. If future assessments are required, the Summary of ADHD Assessments allows for a comparison of evaluation results and can be helpful in determining the relative functioning of the student over time. Copies of the assessment summary should be given to the parents for their personal use and to take to the doctor or be sent to the doctor with their permission. The summary should be discussed with the student whose age and level of maturity indicates the ability to understand the information and utilize it appropriately.

INSTRUCTIONS FOR THE THERAPIST

Use the assessment summary to record the indicators or results from various ADHD assessment tools and informal data collection. Several common rating scales have been listed, and a space has been provided for the results of these tests. Record the information at the top of the form and indicate who completed each assessment tool used (e.g., which parent, family member, or teacher). The assessments are divided into those completed by parents and those completed by school staff. There is an area reserved for additional or alternative testing that may be preferred and routinely used by the school for the ADHD assessment process.

An area is designated for information gathered by the assessment staff from the cumulative record, by a classroom observation, and from contact with the student. Additional comments can be recorded in this area as well. If the information is too long for the space provided, additional pages can be attached. The Summary of ADHD Assessments is designed to provide a concise summary for the parents, doctor, private therapist, or educator who is trying to evaluate the data gathered from the assessment. Longer reports or protocols themselves should be made available upon request.

SUMMARY OF ADHD ASSESSMENTS

Protocols available upon request

Student: _____   Grade: _____

Physician: _____   Phone: _____

Parent(s): _____   Phone: _____

Dates of assessment: from _____   to _____

Report completed by _____   Position: _____

ASSESSMENTS COMPLETED BY PARENT(S)

Scale or Assessment	**Indication or Results**
• Hawthorn ADHD Evaluation Scale (ADDES by McCarney) Completed by _____	_____ _____ _____ _____
• Connors Rating Scale (CSR-R) Completed by _____	_____ _____ _____
• ACTeRS ADD-H Comprehensive Scale Completed by _____	_____ _____ _____
• Informal Symptom Questionnaire Completed by _____	_____ _____ _____

- Other testing used   Completed by

_____   _____   _____

_____   _____   _____

_____   _____   _____

_____   _____   _____

_____   _____   _____

ASSESSMENTS COMPLETED BY SCHOOL STAFF

Scale or Assessment   **Indication or Results**

- Hawthorn ADDES Rating Form
  (ADDES by McCarney)   _____

  Completed by   _____

  _____   _____

                                           _____

- Connors Rating Scale (CSR-R)   _____
  Completed by   _____

  _____   _____

  _____   _____

- ACTeRS ADD-H Comprehensive Scale   _____
  Completed by   _____

  _____   _____

  _____   _____

- *DSM-5* Diagnostic Criteria   _____
  Completed by   _____

  _____   _____

  _____   _____

- Informal Symptom Questionnaire   _____
  Completed by   _____

  _____   _____

  _____   _____

- Other testing used   Completed by

_____   _____   _____

_____   _____   _____

_____   _____   _____

_____   _____   _____

_____   _____   _____

_____   _____   _____

INFORMATION FROM SCHOOL SOCIAL WORKER, COUNSELOR, PSYCHOLOGIST, OR OTHER EDUCATIONAL STAFF

Cumulative record perusal:

_____

_____

_____

_____

Classroom observation:

_____

_____

_____

_____

Contact with the student:

_____

_____

_____

_____

Additional comments:

_____

_____

_____

_____

MEDICATION-MONITORING CHECKLIST

GOALS OF THE EXERCISE

1. Monitor the student's behavioral changes resulting from taking medication.
2. Record any negative side effects caused by the medication.
3. Establish communication between school, home, and the physician regarding the student's reaction to taking the medication.
4. Gather information that can be used by the physician and parents to determine if changes in medication or dosage are warranted.

ADDITIONAL PROBLEMS FOR WHICH THIS EXERCISE MAY BE MOST USEFUL

- Academic Motivation
- Anxiety Reduction
- Assessment for Special Services
- Learning Difficulties

SUGGESTIONS FOR USING THIS EXERCISE WITH STUDENT(S)

When a student is taking medication to correct such conditions as ADHD and other emotional, behavioral, or neurological functioning, significant changes in behavior are often observed by the counselor, social worker, teachers, school staff, parents, and by the student. The Medication-Monitoring Checklist forms for school and home provide an effective method of identifying the effects of medication on the student and commu-nicating these important observations to school staff, parents, and the prescribing physician.

Two forms are available: one for the school to use, for monitoring behavioral changes and reactions to the medication in several important areas, and a similar form for the parents to use. Monitoring should take place for several weeks after the initial prescription of medication by the student's physician and then again several times throughout the year as requested by the doctor or as significant changes in behavior are noted by school staff, the parents, or the student.

The importance of monitoring medication should not be underestimated. As the student matures and grows physically, medications will have different effects on his or her behavior, alertness, mental, and socioemotional functioning. The prescribing physician relies on reports from school and home to determine what changes in medication and dosage are indicated. The Medication-Monitoring Checklist forms provide concrete, observable data that the physician can rely on to make this determination.

MEDICATION-MONITORING CHECKLIST

☐ PARENT FORM (P. 67)

Use the parent form to record any changes you see in your child's behavior, attitude, or habits after he or she begins taking a prescribed medication to treat a physical, behavioral, emotional, or neurological condition. Finding the right dose and type of medication is a process that requires cooperation among the student's family, school, and doctor. Any information that you, your child, and the school can provide will result in a more informed decision by the doctor.

Consider any behavior changes you observe in your child over a two- to three-week period or for the time frame recommended by the doctor. First, record the time frame being reported beside the Dates of Observation line at the top of the checklist, along with the other requested information (e.g., the child's, physician's, and parents' names). Then, rate each behavior change observed at home by checking the appropriate line to indicate whether the behavior is worse, the same, slightly better, or greatly improved since your child began taking the medication. Finally, indicate any side effects you have noted in your child as a result of the medication in the lines found toward the bottom of the form. Your description of any side effects will be especially helpful to the doctor. After the checklist is complete, send it to the doctor or take it with you to your child's next appointment. The school social worker, counselor, or teacher may also find this written documentation useful in his or her efforts to help your child benefit from the prescribed medication.

☐ SCHOOL FORM (P. 69)

Use the school form to record any changes you see in the student's behavior, attitude, or habits after he or she begins taking a prescribed medication to treat a physical, behavioral, emotional, or neurological condition. Finding the right dose and type of medication is a process that requires cooperation among the student's family, school, and doctor. Any information that you, the student, and the parents can provide will result in a more informed decision by the doctor.

Consider any behavior changes you observe in the student over a two- to three-week period or for the time frame recommended by the doctor. First, record the time frame being reported beside the Dates of Observation line at the top of the checklist, along with the other requested information (e.g., the student's, physician's, and parents' names). Then, rate each behavior change observed at school by checking the appropriate line to indicate whether the behavior is worse, the same, slightly better, or greatly improved since the student began taking the medication. Finally, indicate any side effects you have noted in the student as a result of the medication in the lines found toward the bottom of the form. Your description of any side effects will be especially helpful to the doctor. After the checklist is complete, give it to the parents or send it directly to the doctor.

MEDICATION-MONITORING CHECKLIST

PARENT FORM

Child's Name: _____   Grade: _____

Physician: _____   Phone: _____

Parent(s): _____   Phone: _____

Dates of Observation: from _____   to _____

Report completed by _____   Relationship to child: _____

Medication	Dosage	Time Taken	Given by
_____	_____	_____	_____
_____	_____	_____	_____
_____	_____	_____	_____
_____	_____	_____	_____
_____	_____	_____	_____

BEHAVIOR CHANGES OBSERVED AT HOME

Behavior	Worse	Same	Slightly Better	Greatly Improved
Time on task:	_____	_____	_____	_____
Attentive listening:	_____	_____	_____	_____
Work completion:	_____	_____	_____	_____
Talking out:	_____	_____	_____	_____
Cooperation:	_____	_____	_____	_____
Loses things:	_____	_____	_____	_____
Works quietly:	_____	_____	_____	_____
Fidgets or squirms:	_____	_____	_____	_____
Waits for turn:	_____	_____	_____	_____
Finishes task:	_____	_____	_____	_____
High risk-taking:	_____	_____	_____	_____

Behavior	Worse	Same	Slightly Better	Greatly Improved
Talks excessively:	_____	_____	_____	_____
Interrupts:	_____	_____	_____	_____
Organization:	_____	_____	_____	_____
Follows directions:	_____	_____	_____	_____

REACTIONS TO THE MEDICATION OBSERVED BY THE PARENT(S) OR REPORTED BY THE CHILD OR THE SCHOOL

Reaction	Description of Reaction	Time Noted
Sadness	_____	_____
Irritability	_____	_____
Tics or mannerisms	_____	_____
Loss of appetite	_____	_____
Listless or tired	_____	_____
Headaches	_____	_____
Daydreaming	_____	_____
Nervousness	_____	_____
Sleep loss	_____	_____
Other	_____	_____

MEDICATION-MONITORING CHECKLIST

SCHOOL FORM

Student: _____ Grade: _____

Physician: _____ Phone: _____

Parent(s): _____ Phone: _____

Dates of Observation: from _____ to _____

Report completed by _____ Position: _____

Medication	Dosage	Time Taken	Given by
_____	_____	_____	_____
_____	_____	_____	_____
_____	_____	_____	_____
_____	_____	_____	_____
_____	_____	_____	_____

BEHAVIOR CHANGES OBSERVED IN SCHOOL

Behavior	Worse	Same	Slightly Better	Greatly Improved
Time on task:	_____	_____	_____	_____
Attentive listening:	_____	_____	_____	_____
Work completion:	_____	_____	_____	_____
Talking out:	_____	_____	_____	_____
Cooperation:	_____	_____	_____	_____
Loses things:	_____	_____	_____	_____
Works quietly:	_____	_____	_____	_____
Fidgets or squirms:	_____	_____	_____	_____
Waits for turn:	_____	_____	_____	_____
Finishes task:	_____	_____	_____	_____
High risk-taking:	_____	_____	_____	_____

Behavior	Worse	Same	Slightly Better	Greatly Improved
Talks excessively:	_____	_____	_____	_____
Interrupts:	_____	_____	_____	_____
Organization:	_____	_____	_____	_____
Follows directions:	_____	_____	_____	_____

REACTIONS TO THE MEDICATION OBSERVED BY THE SCHOOL STAFF OR REPORTED BY THE PARENT(S) OR THE STUDENT

Reaction	Description of Reaction	Time Noted
Sadness	_____	_____
Irritability	_____	_____
Tics or mannerisms	_____	_____
Loss of appetite	_____	_____
Listless or tired	_____	_____
Headaches	_____	_____
Daydreaming	_____	_____
Nervousness	_____	_____
Sleep loss	_____	_____
Other	_____	_____

SUSTAINED-ATTENTION-SPAN GRAPH

GOALS OF THE EXERCISE

1. Gain an awareness of time-on-task behavior.
2. Improve ability to remain on task during various activities and assignments.
3. Consider factors that contribute to or detract from focus and concentration.
4. Measure attention span and concentration over a specified period.

ADDITIONAL PROBLEMS FOR WHICH THIS EXERCISE MAY BE MOST USEFUL

- Academic Motivation
- Oppositional Defiant Disorder (ODD)
- Responsible Behavior Training
- Learning Difficulties

SUGGESTIONS FOR USING THIS EXERCISE WITH STUDENT(S)

Self-monitoring is a method of focusing the student's attention on personal actions and frequently results in a positive change in the behavior being monitored. The Sustained-Attention-Span Graph outlines for the student the daily activities that require on-task behavior during a typical school day. The categories listed include listening, independent work, small- and large-group assignments, and additional classes and activities (e.g., music, band, physical education, recess). Assign the student to complete the time-on-task record as the day progresses. Self-timing can be accomplished by using a watch, clock, or timer that will record the student's sustained-attention-span for each activity. The time should be recorded by the student in the space provided beside the activity and under the appropriate day of the week. The recording should not be done by the teacher, as this would diminish the effect of self-monitoring on the student's ability to sustain attention.

The teacher's role should be to guide the student in observing and reporting his or her personal behavior. Younger students will need more assistance with listing the activities to be monitored but should record the focused effort numbers themselves. Calculating the total number of minutes spent on task per day and week may require help from the teacher, or the student can use a calculator. The graph should be colored or shaded in by the student to reflect the time on task accomplished each day of the school week and the total weekly number. The questions asked following the graph are designed to encourage the student to assess factors that contribute to and detract from his or her ability to focus and concentrate.

SUSTAINED-ATTENTION-SPAN GRAPH

(STUDENT SELF-MONITORING TIME-ON-TASK RECORD)

Name: _____   Grade: _____

Teacher(s): _____

Dates of Report: from _____   to _____

Use this record and graph to measure your time on task for one week by breaking down each school day into specific assignments, tasks, and activities. Some activities, such as listening to the teacher, are listed on this sheet. For other activities, write the name of the activity in the first column and then time yourself to measure the length of time you were able to pay attention and keep working on the assignment. When you stop paying attention, get up from your seat, or start to do something else, stop timing yourself, and write the time you spent on task in the column beside the activity and under the current day of the week. At the end of each day, add up your total time on task for that day and color or shade in the graph up to the level of the total minutes you spent listening, concentrating, and working on school assignments and activities. On Friday, total up the on-task minutes for the entire week and record that number in the space provided and on the graph. Answer the questions about factors that influence your concentration, and sign the record once it is complete. Save your weekly self-monitoring charts to track your progress throughout the school year.

ACTIVITY OR TASK   TIME-ON-TASK OR FOCUSED EFFORT

	Mon.	Tues.	Wed.	Thurs.	Fri.
Listening					
To the teacher for directions:	_____	_____	_____	_____	_____
To the teacher for information:	_____	_____	_____	_____	_____
To other students during class:	_____	_____	_____	_____	_____
Discussion:	_____	_____	_____	_____	_____
Independent Work					
(Specify subject or activity.)					
_____	_____	_____	_____	_____	_____
_____	_____	_____	_____	_____	_____

ACTIVITY OR TASK   TIME-ON-TASK OR FOCUSED EFFORT

	Mon.	Tues.	Wed.	Thurs.	Fri.
_____	___	___	___	___	___
_____	___	___	___	___	___
_____	___	___	___	___	___

Small-Group Activity

(Specify subject or activity.)

	Mon.	Tues.	Wed.	Thurs.	Fri.
_____	___	___	___	___	___
_____	___	___	___	___	___
_____	___	___	___	___	___
_____	___	___	___	___	___

Whole-Group Activity

(Specify subject or activity.)

	Mon.	Tues.	Wed.	Thurs.	Fri.
_____	___	___	___	___	___
_____	___	___	___	___	___
_____	___	___	___	___	___
_____	___	___	___	___	___
_____	___	___	___	___	___

Other Assignments, Tasks, or Activities

(Specify subject or activity—e.g., recess, music, physical education.)

	Mon.	Tues.	Wed.	Thurs.	Fri.
_____	___	___	___	___	___
_____	___	___	___	___	___
_____	___	___	___	___	___
_____	___	___	___	___	___
_____	___	___	___	___	___

Add up the total time spent on task each day. Use a calculator or get assistance from your teacher if necessary. Record the totals in the following spaces:

	Mon.	Tues.	Wed.	Thurs.	Fri.
_____	___	___	___	___	___

Which day did you spend the most time focused on instruction, tasks, and activities in school? _____

Which day did you focus the least on instruction, tasks, and activities in school?

_____

The activity I focused best on this week was _____

The activity I had the most difficulty focusing on this week was _____

Now add up your total time on task for this week: _____

TIME-ON-TASK GRAPH

Record your time on task each day and for the total week on the following graph by coloring or shading in the rectangles.

Time On Task (min.)	Mon.	Tues.	Wed.	Thurs.	Fri.	Weekly Total
300						
270						
240						
210						
180						
150						
120						
90						
60						
30						

I am most focused and on task when I _____

_____

I am least focused and off task when I _____

_____

Student's signature: _____

Date: _____

Teacher's signature: _____

Teacher's comments: _____

_____

_____

_____

_____

CRITICISM, PRAISE, AND ENCOURAGEMENT

GOALS OF THE EXERCISE

1. Differentiate between personal behavior that attracts encouragement and behavior that attracts criticism.
2. Recognize feelings associated with criticism, praise, and encouragement.
3. Determine proactive methods of seeking encouragement.
4. Identify significant people who frequently give encouragement.

ADDITIONAL PROBLEMS FOR WHICH THIS EXERCISE MAY BE MOST USEFUL

- Academic Motivation
- Oppositional Defiant Disorder (ODD)
- Divorce
- Learning Difficulties
- Blended Family

SUGGESTIONS FOR USING THIS EXERCISE WITH STUDENT(S)

Students are constantly exposed to criticism, praise, and encouragement from their teachers, family members, and peers. These reactions to the student's behavior are often translated into an internal image of the self or the self-concept. Encouragement and specific, descriptive, or appreciative praise each contribute to healthy self-esteem, whereas criticism often demeans the student and deflates the self-image.

Learning how to handle criticism and praise and how to seek encouragement will help the student to develop a more positive self-image and satisfy his or her needs for attention and recognition. The activity asks the student to recognize how criticism, specific praise, encouragement, and being ignored all influence personal feelings. Most students engage in some behavior that attracts encouragement and other behavior that attracts criticism. The activity directs the student to differentiate between personal behaviors that invite positive, encouraging responses from others and those that invite negative, critical responses. The student is assigned to determine some appropriate methods of seeking the encouragement and support he or she needs for feeling recognized and developing the confidence necessary for success in various areas of accomplishment. This activity is appropriate for students in grades kindergarten through 7 and can be adapted for use with older students.

CRITICISM, PRAISE, AND ENCOURAGEMENT

Criticism, praise, and encouragement are different ways that others respond to our behavior. Critical reactions are often associated with negative feelings, whereas specific praise and encouragement promote feelings of pride and a can-do attitude. Choose the word that completes each sentence in the following list or describe your feelings or reactions in your own words.

enjoy	dislike	try harder	discouraged

When I am criticized I feel _____.
Specific praise is something I _____.
When I am encouraged I want to _____.
Being ignored is something I _____.

Every person needs and seeks recognition. Some people gain recognition through misbehavior that attracts criticism; others, through positive behavior that attracts specific praise and encouragement. List some behaviors that gain positive and negative recognition.

Behavior That Attracts Encouragement   **Behavior That Attracts Criticism**

_____   _____

_____   _____

_____   _____

You can replace negative attention or criticism with positive recognition and encouragement by choosing behaviors that attract a positive response from others. Determine which personal behaviors work best to gain positive recognition and record your plan in the spaces provided.

Next time I need some encouragement, I plan to _____

_____

_____

_____

ENCOURAGEMENT VERSUS CRITICISM

The people in our lives respond to us in both positive and negative ways. When they give us encouragement, it helps us to feel recognized, lovable, and capable. Think of a time when you were given encouragement. Draw a picture of that time when an important person in your life (family member, relative, friend, teacher, or mentor) gave you encouragement. Show how you feel when you are encouraged.

Draw a picture of yourself being criticized. Try to remember how you felt and reflect those feelings in your drawing.

POSITIVE VERSUS NEGATIVE ATTENTION-SEEKING BEHAVIOR

GOALS OF THE EXERCISE

1. Recognize that both positive and negative behaviors attract attention.
2. Identify positive and negative personal behavior in various areas of functioning.
3. Establish strategies necessary to redirect negative attention-seeking behavior.
4. Commit to seeking recognition through appropriate behavior.

ADDITIONAL PROBLEMS FOR WHICH THIS EXERCISE MAY BE MOST USEFUL

- Academic Motivation
- Attention-Deficit/Hyperactivity Disorder (ADHD)
- Oppositional Defiant Disorder (ODD)
- Responsible Behavior Training

SUGGESTIONS FOR USING THIS EXERCISE WITH STUDENT(S)

All behavior is goal-directed, and attention is one of the primary goals of students' behavior. However, most students are unaware of the motivations that drive their behaviors. They do not consciously misbehave for negative attention, although this reaction is a powerful reinforcer that supports the constant repetition of the undesirable behavior. Other students behave in positive ways and gain recognition as a result. Positive behavior that attracts recognition and negative behavior that attracts criticism and negative reactions are both attempts by the student to feel important and to fit in or belong to a group.

The Positive versus Negative Attention-Seeking Behavior activity helps the student identify negative behaviors used to gain attention and positive behaviors used for the same purpose. Through brainstorming a list of behaviors in various situations, the student can determine whether most of his or her personal behavior is in the negative or the positive category. Strategies for utilizing more positive behaviors are developed by the student, and a commitment to substitute positive for negative attention-seeking behavior is requested. As the student implements more positive strategies in each area of functioning, these should be recorded on the list as a method of recognizing and reinforcing the student's positive efforts. This activity is appropriate for students in grades 3 through 12 and can be adapted for use with younger students.

POSITIVE VERSUS NEGATIVE ATTENTION-SEEKING BEHAVIOR

All people need attention. Some students gain most of the attention they need through positive behavior (e.g., listening to others, sharing, using manners, studying, doing chores), whereas others choose to get most of their recognition through negative behavior (e.g., bullying, interrupting, breaking rules, not trying, using sarcasm). Most students use a combination of both but favor either a positive or a negative approach. Brainstorm a list of behaviors you use to seek attention in several areas of your life. Compare the two lists and determine if you use primarily positive or negative methods to attract the recognition you need.

Strategies I Use to Seek Attention	Positive Strategies	Negative Strategies
Before school:	*Example: I always get up on time.*	*I have to be called many times.*
	_____	_____
	_____	_____
	_____	_____
	_____	_____
In class:	*Example: I raise my hand to talk.*	*I interrupt others in class.*
	_____	_____
	_____	_____
	_____	_____
	_____	_____
	_____	_____
	_____	_____
	_____	_____

In school, not in class:	*Example: I talk quietly with friends at lunch.*	*I disrupt and throw food in the lunchroom.*
	_____	_____
	_____	_____
	_____	_____
	_____	_____

Strategies I Use to Seek Attention	**Positive Strategies**	**Negative Strategies**
After school:	*Example: I get my homework done.*	*I watch TV and leave the family room a mess.*
	_____	_____
	_____	_____
	_____	_____
	_____	_____
Suppertime:	_____	_____
	_____	_____
Evenings:	_____	_____
	_____	_____
	_____	_____
Bedtime:	_____	_____
	_____	_____
Weekends:	_____	_____
	_____	_____
	_____	_____
Additional times or activities:	_____	_____
	_____	_____
	_____	_____
	_____	_____
	_____	_____

Now that you have completed your list, add up the number of positive methods you use to seek attention and the number of negative methods that you have listed. Record the totals in the following spaces:

Positive Strategies   **Negative Strategies**

_____   _____

Based on my calculation, I get my needs for recognition met by using primarily positive behavior _____, primarily negative behavior _____, or a combination of both _____. (check the appropriate line)

   I can improve my ability to use positive behaviors to get attention by _____

   _____

   _____

   _____

   I can overcome my habit of using negative behaviors to seek recognition by _____

   _____

   _____

   _____

   I am committed to seeking attention and recognition by using appropriate behavior in all areas of my life.

   Signed: _____

   Date: _____

As you begin to use more positive behaviors to get the attention and recognition you need, record these behaviors on your list of strategies in a different color of pen or pencil. Continue adding to the list until all of the positive blanks are filled in. Then you can begin another list if you want to.

MANY ROOMS IN MY HEART

GOALS OF THE EXERCISE

1. Recognize that the heart's capacity to love is unlimited.
2. State positive, loving feelings for first-family and blended-family members.
3. Recognize that loving relationships grow and change.
4. Increase awareness that new relationships do not diminish the love felt for existing relationships.

ADDITIONAL PROBLEMS FOR WHICH THIS EXERCISE MAY BE MOST USEFUL

- Divorce
- Grief and Loss
- Sibling Rivalry
- Parenting Skills/Discipline

SUGGESTIONS FOR USING THIS EXERCISE WITH STUDENT(S)

Many students view their capacity to love as a limited ability. They may even consider it disloyal to develop strong emotional ties to another person for fear that it might diminish their love for those who are currently so important in their lives. This is especially true when children are faced with a divorce followed by the formation of a blended family, which combines members of their first family and, as a result of remarriage of their parents, additional family members.

This activity demonstrates to the student that his or her heart is an extremely flexible organ that can grow and expand to make room for all the loving relationships that enter his or her life. The rooms in the heart are designated by lines where the student can enter the names of first-family members, blended-family members, extended-first and blended-family members, and others he or she loves or will love in the future. The student is asked to fill in as many lines as possible with existing loving relationships and to save any remaining lines for future significant others in his or her life. If the student should fill in all of the rooms in the heart, ask him or her to draw another heart large enough to include all of the names representing close family and other personal relationships. This activity is appropriate for students in grades 3 through 12 and can be adapted for use with younger students.

MANY ROOMS IN MY HEART

Our heart is an organ that grows and expands to accept and surround each new person that we love. There is no limit to our capacity to love; our heart cannot become too full of people we care about, for instead of breaking, it becomes stronger as each room is filled with a new person to love. Begin this activity by connecting the dots to draw a heart. Then list all the members of your first family (mother, father, brothers, and sisters) and add extended members of your first family (e.g., grandparents, aunts, uncles, cousins). Use the additional rooms beside the first-family members if necessary. Next, add the new members of your blended family, as well as the extended blended-family members, by using the adjacent additional rooms lines. Note that there are still many rooms left in your heart for other people in your life whom you love and for people whom you will love in the future. Fill in these rooms now with the names of people that you currently care about, and save any additional rooms for future relationships. Don't worry if you run out of rooms; you can always draw a bigger heart.

Additional Rooms   **First Family Members**   **Blended Family Members**   **Additional Rooms**

_____   _____   _____   _____

_____   _____   _____   _____

_____   _____   _____   _____

_____   _____   _____   _____

_____   _____   _____   _____

_____   _____   _____   _____

Rooms for Others I Love or Will Love in the Future

_____

_____

_____

_____

_____

_____

_____

NEW PEOPLE IN MY FAMILY

GOALS OF THE EXERCISE

1. Define how the family has changed from the original to a blended family.
2. State positive feelings for blended-family members.
3. View forming a relationship with blended-family members as an ongoing process.
4. Recognize the many relationships that exist in a blended family.

ADDITIONAL PROBLEMS FOR WHICH THIS EXERCISE MAY BE MOST USEFUL

- Divorce
- Grief/Loss
- Sibling Rivalry
- Parenting Skills/Discipline

SUGGESTIONS FOR USING THIS EXERCISE WITH STUDENT(S)

Students are often confused and anxious about their relationship to various members of their blended family or families. Today's family evolves many times over the life of the student, and it is often difficult for the student to define the existing family and how each person fits into the newly formed group. The New People in My Family activity asks the student to identify and describe each blended family member (e.g., stepparents, stepsiblings, stepgrandparents, special uncles, aunts, and cousins). This process will clarify the relationships for the student and help him or her begin to accept the stepfamily members and relate to them appropriately and productively.

The student is encouraged to view the process of getting to know stepfamily members in a positive manner by identifying aspects of the new family member that they like, aspects that surprise them, and aspects they want to know more about. Drawing pictures or entering photos of each blended-family member helps the student to accept the relationships as a reality that must be dealt with. The student is instructed to compare his or her current family with his or her first family in picture form and to record some thoughts and feelings about each family group. This activity can lead to therapeutic discussions regarding the student's adjustment to the new family, as well as areas of conflict or distress and areas of growth in accepting the very different family setting. The activity can become a part of a personal journal kept by the student to record his or her ongoing blended family issues. This activity is appropriate for students in grades 3 through 12 and can be adapted for use with younger students.

NEW PEOPLE IN MY FAMILY

When parents remarry, our families often grow and change. New people join our family, and suddenly we have stepfathers or stepmothers, stepbrothers, stepsisters, stepgrandparents, and other extended stepfamily members (e.g., aunts, uncles, cousins). This new family combination is called a *blended family*, because members from your first family are blended with members from your new stepfather's or stepmother's family. Sometimes this change takes a little time to get used to. Living with or just getting to know and understand new members of the blended family can seem rather strange and difficult at first.

Work on accepting and getting to know your new family by describing each person in the following lines and then drawing a picture of them or pasting a photo in the space provided. When you have completed your descriptions, record a picture of your first family and your blended family. If you are a member of two blended families (both your father and mother have remarried), complete this activity for each of your blended families.

Name of my new stepparent: _____

Description: _____

_____

_____

_____

_____

Something I want to learn about my new stepparent: _____

_____

Something that surprised me about my new stepparent: _____

_____

Something I really like about my new stepparent: _____

_____

Draw a picture or paste a photo of you and your stepparent in the box provided.

```



```

Name of my new stepbrother(s) or stepsister(s): _____
_____
_____

Description: _____
_____
_____
_____
_____

Something I want to learn about my new stepsibling(s): _____
_____

Something that surprised me about my new stepsibling(s): _____
_____

Something I really like about my new stepsibling(s): _____
_____

Draw a picture or paste a photo of you and your stepsibling(s) in the box provided.

Name of my new stepgrandparent(s): _____

_____

Description: _____

_____

_____

_____

_____

Something I want to learn about my new stepgrandparent(s): _____

_____

Something that surprised me about my new stepgrandparent(s): _____

_____

Something I really like about my new stepgrandparent(s): _____

_____

Draw a picture or paste a photo of you and your stepgrandparent(s) in the box provided.

Name of another special blended family member (aunt, uncle, cousin, etc.): _____

_____

Description: _____

_____

_____

_____

_____

Something I want to learn about this special person: _____

_____

Something that surprised me about this special person: _____

_____

Something I really like about this special person: _____

_____

Draw a picture or paste a photo of you and a special blended family member in the box provided.

Use additional pages if you have more than one special blended family member to describe or illustrate.

Draw a picture or paste a photo of you and your first family as it was before your parents' separation.

Something I would like to say about my first family: _____

_____

_____

_____

_____

_____

_____

_____

_____

Draw a picture or paste a photo of you and your blended family as it is right now.

Something I would like to say about my blended family: _____

_____

_____

_____

_____

_____

_____

_____

_____

BULLYING INCIDENT REPORT

GOALS OF THE EXERCISE*

1. Identify contributing factors and sequence of events that led up to bullying or threatening behavior at home, school, or in the community.
2. Explore underlying emotions that contribute to bullying or intimidating behavior at home, school, or in the community.
3. Express hurt and anger in nonviolent ways.
4. Terminate intimidating behavior and treat others with respect and kindness.

ADDITIONAL PROBLEMS FOR WHICH THIS EXERCISE MAY BE MOST USEFUL

- Anger Management
- Depression
- Oppositional Defiant

SUGGESTIONS FOR PROCESSING THIS EXERCISE WITH THE CLIENT

The incident report in this assignment should be completed by the client shortly after engaging in an act of bullying or intimidation at home, school, or in the neighborhood. The student's responses to the questionnaire will hopefully provide insight into the factors or sequence of events that led up to his or her bullying or intimidating behavior. The student is asked to identify the underlying emotions that he or she was experiencing prior to the bullying incident. It is hoped that the student will learn other more adaptive ways to express and/or manage his or her anger other than behaving in an intimidating or bullying manner. It is acceptable for teachers or other school officials to help the student complete the questionnaire if this behavior occurred at school.

* This exercise originates from Jongsma, A. E., Peterson, L. M., & McInnis, W. P. (in press). *Child Psychotherapy Homework Planner* (5th ed.). Hoboken, NJ: Wiley. Reprinted with permission.

BULLYING INCIDENT REPORT

1. Date of incident: _____

   Approximate time: _____

   Place or setting: _____

2. Please describe the incident when you either bullied or threatened someone. _____
   _____
   _____

3. What events led up to you bullying or threatening the other child or children? _____
   _____
   _____

4. What had your mood and behavior been like the day before the incident? (Check all that apply.)

   ___ Angry or mad   ___ Fearful   ___ Quiet and withdrawn

   ___ Irritable or grouchy   ___ Guilty   ___ Disappointed

   ___ Frustrated   ___ Happy   ___ Bored

   ___ Lonely   ___ Content or satisfied   ___ Embarrassed

   ___ Felt unwanted   ___ Hyperactive   ___ Other (please identify)

   ___ Nervous   ___ Sad

   ___ Worried

5. What thoughts did you experience before you made the threats or bullied the other child or children? _____
   _____

6. What were the consequences of your behavior for the other child or children? What bad things happened to them? _____
   _____

7. How did other kids react to your threatening or bullying behavior? _____
   _____

8. How did the teachers, school officials, or parents of the other child or children react to your threatening or bullying behavior? _____

_____

9. How did your parents react to your threatening or bullying behavior? _____

_____

10. What punishment did you receive at home or school because of your threatening or bullying behavior? _____

_____

11. What other things could you do in the future to control your anger and stop acting like a bully? (Please check all that apply.)

_____ Walk away before bullying others

_____ Ignore teasing, name-calling, or mean remarks

_____ Talk calmly to other kid(s) about the problem

_____ Listen better to other kid(s) with whom I am angry

_____ Find physical ways to express anger (e.g., play sports, run)

_____ Express anger by writing in journal

_____ Express anger through drawings

_____ Talk to friends or other kids about the problem

_____ Talk to parents, school counselor, or teacher

_____ Meet with other kids involved in incident and grown-ups to talk about the problem

_____ Other (please identify) _____

12. If you had to do it all over again, how would you have handled the incident differently?

_____

_____

_____

APOLOGY LETTER FOR BULLYING

GOALS OF THE EXERCISE*

1. Offer sincere and genuine apology to other children who have been victims of the bullying, threatening, or intimidating behavior.
2. Verbalize an acceptance of responsibility for bullying or intimidating behavior.
3. Develop empathy and compassion for others.
4. Terminate intimidating behavior and treat others with respect and kindness.

ADDITIONAL PROBLEMS FOR WHICH THIS EXERCISE MAY BE MOST USEFUL

- Anger Management
- Conduct Disorder/Delinquency
- Peer/Sibling Conflict

SUGGESTIONS FOR PROCESSING THIS EXERCISE WITH THE CLIENT

The purpose of this assignment is to prepare the client to offer a sincere, genuine apology to the other child (or children) who has been a victim of his or her bullying, threatening, or intimidating behavior. The student is first required to respond to a series of questions or items that will help him or her offer a well-thought-out apology. After responding to the questions, the client is encouraged to write a rough draft on a separate piece of paper. The student should share and process the contents of the rough draft with the therapist before giving a sincere apology to the victim(s). The counselor should explore whether the client should give either a verbal or written apology. One of the primary goals of the exercise is to increase the student's empathy and sensitivity to how his or her aggressive and threatening behavior may negatively impact others. The counselor should challenge or confront any statements in which the client projects the blame for his or her bullying or threatening behavior onto other people or outside circumstances and refuses to accept full responsibility.

---

* This exercise originates from Jongsma, A. E., Peterson, L. M., & McInnis, W. P. (in press). *Child Psychotherapy Homework Planner* (5th ed.). Hoboken, NJ: Wiley. Reprinted with permission.

APOLOGY LETTER FOR BULLYING

You are being asked to apologize to _____ who you have either
(Name of child/other children)
bullied, threatened, or frightened in some way. Before giving your apology, please respond to the following questions or items. Your answers or responses will help you give a well-thought-out apology and show that you are truly sorry for your bullying or threatening behavior.

1. Please describe your bullying or threatening behavior. _____
   _____
   _____
   _____

2. What were the reasons or factors that caused you to either bully or threaten the other child or children? _____
   _____
   _____

3. Tell in your own words why you are responsible or at fault for your bullying or threatening behavior. _____
   _____
   _____
   _____

4. Now tell the reasons why the other child or children are not responsible or to blame for your bullying or threatening behavior. _____
   _____
   _____

5. What bad things happened to the other child or children as a result of your bullying or threatening behavior? Was the other child physically hurt or emotionally upset? Please describe. _____
   _____
   _____

6. What punishment did you receive, either at home or school, because of your bullying or threatening behavior? _____

_____

_____

7. How has your bullying or threatening behavior affected your relationship with the other child or children involved in the incident? _____

_____

_____

8. What lessons have you learned about how your bullying behavior affects others? ___

_____

_____

9. What can you say to the other child or children that shows that you have accepted your punishment? _____

_____

_____

10. What can you say to the other child or children that will help them feel better or safer in the future? _____

_____

_____

On a separate piece of paper, write a rough draft of your apology to the other child or children. Look back over your responses or answers to the previous questions to help write your letter. Do not send the rough draft or give an apology to the other child or children without first talking to your counselor. Please bring your responses and rough draft to the next counseling session.

PROBLEM-SOLVING: AN ALTERNATIVE TO IMPULSIVE ACTION

GOALS OF THE EXERCISE*

1. Identify the specific ADD behaviors that cause the most difficulty.
2. List the negative consequences of the ADD problematic behavior.
3. Apply problem-solving skills to specific ADD behaviors that are interfering with daily functioning.

ADDITIONAL PROBLEMS FOR WHICH THIS EXERCISE MAY BE MOST USEFUL

- Anger Management
- Bipolar – Mania
- Impulse Control Disorder

SUGGESTIONS FOR PROCESSING THIS EXERCISE WITH THE CLIENT

Students with Attention Deficit Disorder (ADD) are characterized by their tendency to exercise poor judgment and act without considering the consequences of their actions. The ADD client frequently finds him- or herself in trouble without realizing what caused him or her to get there and fails to recognize the antecedents of his or her negative consequences. In this exercise, the student is taught a basic problem-solving strategy to help inhibit impulses. The student first identifies a problem with impulsivity and then works through the subsequent problem-solving stages. This exercise can be used with students who do not have ADD but do have problems with impulse control.

---

* This exercise originates from Jongsma, A. E., Peterson, L. M., & McInnis, W. P. (in press). *Adult Psychotherapy Homework Planner* (5th ed.). Hoboken, NJ: Wiley. Reprinted with permission.

PROBLEM-SOLVING: AN ALTERNATIVE TO IMPULSIVE ACTION

Students with Attention Deficit Disorder (ADD) often find themselves in trouble without realizing what caused them to get there. It is not uncommon for students with ADD to try to solve problems by quickly rushing into a situation without stopping and thinking about the possible consequences of their actions. The failure to stop and think causes negative consequences for both self and others. If this sounds all too familiar to you, and you are tired of finding yourself in trouble because of your failure to stop and think, then this exercise is designed for you. In this exercise, you are taught to use basic problem-solving steps to deal with a stressful situation. By following these steps, you will hopefully find yourself in less trouble with others and feel better about yourself.

1. The first step in solving any problem is to realize that a problem exists. At this beginning stage, you are asked to identify either a major impulsivity problem that you are currently facing or a common reoccurring problem that troubles you and is caused by your impulsive actions.

    Identify the problem. _____

    _____

2. After identifying the problem, consider three different alternative possible courses of action to help you solve or deal with the impulsivity problem. List the pros and cons of each possible course of action. Record at least three different pros and cons for each course of action.

    First possible course of action to be taken: _____

    _____

    Pros _____   **Cons** _____

    _____   _____

    _____   _____

    _____   _____

    Second possible course of action to be taken: _____

    _____

Pros _____   **Cons** _____

_____   _____

_____   _____

_____   _____

Third possible course of action to be taken: _____

Pros _____   **Cons** _____

_____   _____

_____   _____

_____   _____

3. Next, review the pros and cons of each one of your possible courses of action. At this point, talk with your partner, a family member, a friend, or a peer to help you choose a final plan of action.

4. Identify the course of action that you plan to follow. _____

_____

5. What factors influenced you to choose this course of action? _____

_____

_____

6. What advice or input did you receive from others that influenced your decision? ___

_____

_____

Now you are in the final stage of this exercise. You have identified the problem, considered different possible courses of action, made a decision, and followed through on your plan of action. Your final task is to evaluate the results or success of your plan of action. Please respond to the following questions.

7. What were the results of your plan of action? _____

_____

8. How do you feel about the results? _____

_____

_____

9. How did your plan affect both you and others? _____

_____

_____

10. What did you learn from this experience? _____

_____

_____

_____

11. What, if anything, would you do differently if you were faced with the same or a similar problem in the future? _____

_____

_____

_____

ATTRIBUTES FOR A SUCCESSFUL CAREER

GOALS OF THE EXERCISE

1. Verbalize an understanding of personal attributes.
2. Describe positive work habits required for success in school and future jobs.
3. Identify existing positive personal attributes that contribute to success in school.
4. Define situations at school and work that require specific positive work habits.

ADDITIONAL PROBLEMS FOR WHICH THIS EXERCISE MAY BE MOST USEFUL

- Academic Motivation
- Attachment/Bonding Deficits
- Learning Difficulties
- Responsible Behavior Training

SUGGESTIONS FOR USING THIS EXERCISE WITH STUDENT(S)

Students frequently view school and work as two completely separate entities when, in actuality, school is a training ground that prepares students for the world of work. The Attributes for a Successful Career activity helps students understand that the personal qualities that help them to be successful at school are often the same attributes that employers seek in their future employees.

This activity can be done alone with the counselor but is probably more effective when steps 1, 2, and 3 are completed in a group or as a classroom activity and steps 4 and 5 are completed individually by the student. The group or classroom is asked to brainstorm a list of habits or attributes that contribute to success in school, in the workplace, and in both settings. When the list is complete, students are asked to differentiate those qualities that pertain to school and to work and those that will enhance effectiveness in both environments.

First, the students are directed to consider several scenarios from the school setting and the workplace and choose an attribute that will contribute to a positive result in each situation. Then, the students are directed to design some of their own scenarios based on personal experience. Finally, each student is asked to identify several personal attributes they now have and to determine those attributes that need to be developed to promote their efficiency and effectiveness in school and in future employment. The activity will help each student to assess his or her existing personal habits and evaluate those attributes that need to be developed to prepare for a successful career. This activity is appropriate for students in grades 5 through 12 and can be adapted for use with younger students.

ATTRIBUTES FOR A SUCCESSFUL CAREER

SCENARIOS OF CONFLICT TO ROLE-PLAY, BRAINSTORM, AND RESOLVE

Many of the qualities that help you to be successful at school will also help you when you get a job, go to college, take some skill training, or prepare for a profession. These qualities, called *personal attributes*, include such characteristics as patience, persistence, communication skills, personal hygiene, promptness, and cooperation.

1. Brainstorm with your classmates, group members, parents, or counselor a list of personal qualities that will help you and your classmates to be successful either at school or in a career. Put an S next to the qualities that apply only to *school* and a W next to the qualities that apply only at *work*. Place a B next to the qualities that are important for *both* school and work.

    _____   _____   _____

    _____   _____   _____

    _____   _____   _____

    _____   _____   _____

    _____   _____   _____

2. Work with your classmates to select one or more of the preceding attributes to complete the following sentences. If you don't find an attribute that fits the situation, add one of your own.

    When I am participating in a class or group discussion, an important attribute to use is _____

    _____

    When playing a game at recess or in physical education, an important attribute to use is _____

    _____

    When I am preparing for a test, exam, or quiz, an important attribute to use is ___

    _____

    When I am practicing for a band concert, an important attribute to use is _____

    _____

    When I apply for my first job, an important attribute to demonstrate will be _____

    _____

When I ask for a raise in salary or a promotion, an important attribute to demonstrate will be _____

When I'm problem solving with my coworkers, an important attribute to demonstrate will be _____

When my boss is evaluating my work, an important attribute to demonstrate will be _____

When I'm frustrated and need help to solve a problem, an important attribute to demonstrate is _____

When I feel left out, ignored, or unappreciated, an important attribute to demonstrate is _____

When I lose a game, contest, or competition, an important attribute to demonstrate is _____

3. Continue working with your classmates to design some scenarios in which positive personal attributes will contribute to a successful outcome.

    When _____ , an important attribute to demonstrate is _____

    When _____ , an important attribute to demonstrate is _____

    When _____ , an important attribute to demonstrate is _____

    When _____ , an important attribute to demonstrate is _____

4. Working alone, now consider the personal attributes that help you to succeed in school. List six of these personal attributes in the lines provided.

    Some attributes I have that help me to be successful at school are

    _____   _____   _____

    _____   _____   _____

5. List some of the personal attributes that will help you when you are working on a job or in a profession.

    Some attributes I have that will help me to be successful at work are

    _____   _____   _____

    _____   _____   _____

    Think about some additional attributes that would help you to increase your success at school and will help you in the future when you are working. List these personal attributes in the lines provided.

    Some attributes I want to develop to help me become more successful at school and work are

    _____   _____   _____

    _____   _____   _____

    _____   _____   _____

CAREERS FOR A LIFETIME

GOALS OF THE EXERCISE

1. Develop an awareness of the occupations held by community members of various ages.
2. View the world of work as a dynamic entity that changes over the course of the lifetime.
3. Select several occupational possibilities to pursue during future working years.
4. Recognize that work and productivity is an ongoing, lifelong process.

ADDITIONAL PROBLEMS FOR WHICH THIS EXERCISE MAY BE MOST USEFUL

- Academic Motivation
- Attachment/Bonding Deficits
- Learning Difficulties
- Responsible Behavior Training

SUGGESTIONS FOR USING THIS EXERCISE WITH STUDENT(S)

The probability of the student being involved with several jobs, occupations, or careers during the course of his or her working life is very high. The question is no longer which occupation to pursue after graduation from college or high school but, rather, which several career options will be pursued. The Careers for a Lifetime activity asks the student to observe and/or interview various family and community members, focusing on their career choices and the jobs they have held during different stages of their lives. Then, the student brainstorms with other classmates or group members about various jobs held by people in the early, middle, and late stages of their working years. Finally, the student is directed to independently consider what types of professions or occupations he or she might pursue in the course of his or her own lifetime.

The activity encourages the student to develop an awareness of career options and the choices that people familiar to him or her have made. Work and productivity are portrayed as an ongoing, lifelong process that extends from the teen years through the postretirement years. The student's view of work is expanded, and personal career choices become an open-ended series of opportunities rather than a restricted decision limited to only one option. This activity can be used with students in the later elementary grades through high school.

CAREERS FOR A LIFETIME

During your lifetime you will probably have several jobs and careers, beginning in your teen years and extending well into your postretirement years. Consider the various jobs held by your own siblings, parents, grandparents, and extended family members. What different types of jobs, careers, and work-related activities have they participated in? If you're not sure of the specific jobs and work done by your family members and other adults in the community, interview people from various age groups to determine the types of careers chosen by them at different stages of their lives.

1. Work with a group of classmates to brainstorm several jobs, occupations, and productive activities chosen by people you are familiar with during the different ages and stages of their lives.

Jobs and Productive Activities Chosen by Teenagers

_____   _____   _____

_____   _____   _____

_____   _____   _____

_____   _____   _____

Jobs and Productive Activities Chosen by Young Adults 20–30

_____   _____   _____

_____   _____   _____

_____   _____   _____

_____   _____   _____

Jobs and Productive Activities Chosen by Adults 30–40

_____   _____   _____

_____   _____   _____

_____   _____   _____

_____   _____   _____

Jobs and Productive Activities Chosen by Adults 40–60

_____ _____ _____
_____ _____ _____
_____ _____ _____
_____ _____ _____

Jobs and Productive Activities Chosen by Adults 60–70

_____ _____ _____
_____ _____ _____
_____ _____ _____
_____ _____ _____

Jobs and Productive Activities Chosen by Adults 70 and Older

_____ _____ _____
_____ _____ _____
_____ _____ _____
_____ _____ _____

2. Working alone, list some of the jobs you hope to consider during the stages of your own lifetime.

My first job will probably be

_____ or _____ or _____

After I graduate, I would like to

_____ or _____ or _____

Between 20 and 30, I will pursue a career in

_____ or _____ or _____

Between 40 and 60, I will pursue a career in

_____ or _____ or _____

Between 60 and 70, I will pursue a career in

_____ or _____ or _____

After I retire, the areas in which I would like to pursue work and activities are

_____ or _____ or _____

OCCUPATIONS, TASKS, AND TOOLS

GOALS OF THE EXERCISE

1. List and describe various jobs in the community.
2. Describe the tasks and tools required by specific professions.
3. Verbalize an awareness of why people work.
4. Evaluate several occupations in terms of interest, difficulty, and value to the community.

ADDITIONAL PROBLEMS FOR WHICH THIS EXERCISE MAY BE MOST USEFUL

- Academic Motivation
- Attachment/Bonding Deficits
- Learning Difficulties
- Responsible Behavior Training

SUGGESTIONS FOR USING THIS EXERCISE WITH STUDENT(S)

Career awareness and the school-to-work emphasis should begin early so that students can view school as a stepping-stone to becoming contributing members of the community. The Occupations, Tasks, and Tools activity can be used with students from the early elementary through middle school grades to create an awareness of the occupations and professions that are performed daily by familiar adults in their family and community. As the student begins to comprehend how work directly affects the quality of life and the survival of families in the community, the nation, and the world, an understanding of the connection of the work done in school to future careers and lifestyles will begin to emerge. The activity directs the student to brainstorm a list of various jobs or professions with classmates or with an adult. It then directs the student to work in a group to define several occupations of interest in terms of tasks performed and tools required to complete the work.

This analysis helps the student to evaluate various professions in terms of personal interest, enjoyment, significance to community welfare, and difficulty of the work performed. The activity encourages the student to look at several familiar occupations in more specific, realistic terms and begin to formulate some personal knowledge of work-related interests and aptitude, as well as the desire to pursue particular professions in the future.

OCCUPATIONS, TASKS, AND TOOLS

Think of all the adults that you know with jobs and occupations who support both themselves and others by work that is important and necessary for the survival of their families and their communities. Consider the people in your own family, school, church, and community who work in various professions.

Brainstorm with your classmates, group members, parents, or counselor a list of jobs held by adults in your family and community. List all of the occupations below:

_____   _____   _____

_____   _____   _____

_____   _____   _____

_____   _____   _____

_____   _____   _____

_____   _____   _____

_____   _____   _____

Now select several of these occupations, describe the various tasks performed on the job, and list the tools required to complete the work. Complete this activity with classmates, or interview your parents or other adults to gather as many ideas as possible.

Profession	Type of Work	Tools Required
Examples:		
Carpenter	*Builds or makes things*	*Hammer, saw, nails*
	_____	_____
	_____	_____
	_____	_____
Day Care Provider	*Takes care of children*	*Toys, food, blankets*
	_____	_____
	_____	_____
	_____	_____

Now do some on your own:

Profession	Type of Work	Tools Required
_____	_____	_____
	_____	_____
	_____	_____
	_____	_____
	_____	_____
	_____	_____
_____	_____	_____
	_____	_____
	_____	_____
	_____	_____
	_____	_____
_____	_____	_____
	_____	_____
	_____	_____
	_____	_____
	_____	_____
	_____	_____
_____	_____	_____
	_____	_____
	_____	_____
	_____	_____
	_____	_____
_____	_____	_____
	_____	_____
	_____	_____

_____   _____

_____   _____

_____   _____

_____   _____

_____

_____   _____

_____   _____

_____   _____

_____   _____

_____   _____

_____   _____

_____   _____

_____

_____   _____

_____   _____

_____   _____

_____   _____

List the occupations that you and the other group members consider to be most important to the community.

_____   _____   _____

_____   _____   _____

List the types of work that you and the other group members would like to perform as adults.

_____   _____   _____

_____   _____   _____

List the types of work that you and the other group members consider to be the most difficult.

_____   _____   _____

List the types of work that you and the other group members consider to be the most enjoyable.

_____   _____   _____

FEELINGS VOCABULARY

GOALS OF THE EXERCISE

1. Develop awareness of the many words used to express feelings.
2. View feelings as chosen methods of reacting to events.
3. Identify feelings associated with conflict and problem resolution.
4. Recognize personal feelings that trigger either negative or positive reactions.

ADDITIONAL PROBLEMS FOR WHICH THIS EXERCISE MAY BE MOST USEFUL

*   Anger Management/Aggression
*   Anxiety Reduction
*   Conflict Management
*   Depression
*   Suicide

SUGGESTIONS FOR USING THIS EXERCISE WITH STUDENT(S)

Students often feel controlled or victimized by their feelings. They assume that their feelings control them rather than the other way around and that they lack the ability to determine personal behavioral reactions. The Feelings Vocabulary activity lists feelings that typically occur as an individual interprets and reacts to the events and circumstances in his/her life. The student is asked to read the list of feelings and add some additional feelings experienced personally or by others. This can be done individually or as part of a group brainstorming exercise. The activity will help expand the student's vocabulary and develop awareness of the numerous ways to express personal emotion other than the greatly overused feelings of anger, sadness, and happiness.

Ask the student to identify feelings from the vocabulary list that indicate a positive, peacekeeping attitude and those that are potential precursors of conflict. Personal responses to common scenarios that can trigger various emotional reactions are then completed by the student to develop an awareness of his/her typically chosen feelings. Instruct the student to design several situations that commonly occur in school or at home and record a response that he/she frequently chooses. An awareness of the personal feelings most commonly chosen will alert the student to personal feelings that often trigger conflict, those that are helpful in problem solving and conflict resolution, and those that create a positive, pleasant atmosphere. Instruct the student to define several healthy methods of experiencing more positive emotions. This activity is appropriate for students in grades 5 through 12.

FEELINGS VOCABULARY

What follows is a list of feelings that are commonly experienced by students. Look over the list and add any additional words that represent feelings you are aware of or experience often. Highlight the feelings commonly associated with school violence and conflict. Underline the feelings that express well-being. Place a star next to the feelings that occur just before or that contribute to conflict, but circle the feelings that lead to peaceful resolutions.

Abandoned	Enraged	Lovestruck	Suspicious
Angry	Excited	Loving	Uneasy
Anxious	Exhausted	Mad	Upset
Ashamed	Foolish	Mischievous	Uptight
Badgered	Frightened	Neglected	Victimized
Betrayed	Frustrated	Nervous	Welcome
Bored	Guilty	Overwhelmed	Worried
Calm	Happy	Proud	_____
Cautious	Helpless	Sad	_____
Chippy	Hopeful	Scared	_____
Confident	Hopeless	Serene	_____
Confused	Horrified	Serious	_____
Curious	Hysterical	Shamed	_____
Depressed	Important	Shocked	_____
Disappointed	Jealous	Shy	_____
Disgusted	Lazy	Smart	_____
Ecstatic	Left out	Smug	_____
Embarrassed	Lonely	Surprised	_____

Feelings are created by the way we choose to react to events. We can make a decision to become enraged as a result of something that happened, or we can choose to remain calm and determine how best to deal with the situation.

Use the following scenarios to record various ways you can choose to react emotionally to different situations.

When my friends ignore me, I often choose to feel _____

When my team wins, I often choose to feel _____

When I get teased, I often choose to feel _____

When my parent or teacher criticizes me, I often choose to feel _____

When I receive encouragement, I often choose to feel _____

When my friends ask me to join them, I often choose to feel _____

Now create some scenarios of your own. Record more than one feeling for each situation, if appropriate.

When _____ I often choose to feel _____

When _____ I often choose to feel _____

When _____ I often choose to feel _____

When _____ I often choose to feel _____

When _____ I often choose to feel _____

Next time I experience negative feelings that may lead to a dispute, I will try to remain calm and work on a solution to the problem rather than react emotionally, intensifying the conflict.

Emotions I need to watch for that can contribute to conflicts are

_____   _____   _____

_____   _____   _____

Emotions that can contribute to problem solving and peacemaking are

_____   _____   _____

_____   _____   _____

My most commonly experienced feelings are

_____   _____   _____

_____   _____   _____

Emotions that I would like to experience more often are

_____   _____   _____

_____   _____   _____

Some healthy ways for me to experience more positive emotions are

1. _____

2. _____

3. _____

4. _____

LISTENING SKILLS

GOALS OF THE EXERCISE

1. Verbalize a definition of effective listening.
2. Identify the feelings expressed during a conversation.
3. Acquire techniques that are necessary for becoming an active listener.
4. Acknowledge the credibility of others' feelings.

ADDITIONAL PROBLEMS FOR WHICH THIS EXERCISE MAY BE MOST USEFUL

- Anger Management/Aggression
- Attention-Seeking Behavior
- Conflict Management
- Parenting Skills/Discipline
- Self-Esteem Building
- Social Skills/Peer Relationships

SUGGESTIONS FOR USING THIS EXERCISE WITH STUDENT(S)

Students often view communication with others as self-expression or talking to others. This activity is designed to teach the sometimes forgotten aspect of communication: *listening*. Discuss with the student the three components of active listening: (1) eye contact, (2) paraphrasing, and (3) reflecting the feeling being expressed. Review the feelings listed in the activity that are to be used in identifying the feelings expressed in the examples listed. Then instruct the student to select a feeling that would appropriately reflect the speaker's feelings based on the information given in each example.

The Listening Skills activity provides an opportunity for the student to practice listening with attention and interest. Focusing on the feelings or emotions of the person speaking will allow the student to acknowledge and give credibility to the feelings being expressed. Emotional expression is often the most important component of the message being delivered; however, this aspect of communication is often disregarded or overlooked. The Listening Skills activity encourages the student to become a better listener by responding to the most essential part of the information being delivered. This activity is appropriate for students in grades 3 through 9 and can be adapted for use with older or younger students.

LISTENING SKILLS

Being a good listener is a skill that is developed through a lot of practice. This activity defines the three parts of effective listening and allows you to respond to several situations that require you to listen with concern and caring. Perhaps a friend or family member tells you about something that has made him or her feel sad or unhappy. You would respond with the word that describes the feeling you imagine that they are experiencing. Or, a family member is letting you know about something wonderful that is about to happen. You could let them know that you recognize their excitement by responding with a feeling word that reflects their joy.

Discuss the three parts of being a good listener with your counselor, teacher, or parent; then review the feeling words listed and add any additional words that describe feelings you commonly experience. Finally, complete the responses to a statement from another person by choosing a feeling word that reflects the way they are feeling about an event that is affecting their attitude or emotions. Continue to practice using feeling words to respond to conversations with others and you will find that your family and friends recognize your listening talents and seek you out often to share their feelings and experiences.

A good listener tries to

1. Look at the person who is speaking
2. Remember and be able to repeat back important details
3. Identify how the person is feeling

Read the following list of feeling words and add several of your own:

Angry	Disgusted	Guilty	Overwhelmed
Anxious	Ecstatic	Happy	Sad
Ashamed	Embarrassed	Hopeful	Serious
Bored	Enraged	Hysterical	Shocked
Cautious	Excited	Jealous	Shy
Confident	Exhausted	Lonely	Smug
Confused	Frightened	Lovestruck	Surprised
Depressed	Frustrated	Mischievous	Suspicious

Choose a word from the preceding list that reflects the feeling being communicated in each of the following situations:

Your friend tells you his dog has just died.

Response: You sound very _____

Someone has just told a joke that made you laugh.

Response: That is really _____

A classmate has lost her homework.

Response: You look like you're _____

The teacher is explaining important instructions for the test.

Response: Remain quiet and look _____

A friend tells you she and her parents are going to Disney World.

Response: You must be very _____

Now try a few of your own:

_____

Response: You sound very _____

_____

Response: You sound very _____

_____

Response: You sound very _____

_____

Response: You sound very _____

_____

Response: You sound very _____

Think of some people in your life who would appreciate being listened to with caring and concern. List their names in the following lines:

_____   _____   _____

_____   _____   _____

_____   _____   _____

SPEAKING SKILLS

GOALS OF THE EXERCISE

1. Verbalize strategies for self-expression.
2. Assume responsibility for personal feelings.
3. Express feelings without blaming others or telling them what to do.
4. Develop appropriate assertiveness and self-confidence.

ADDITIONAL PROBLEMS FOR WHICH THIS EXERCISE MAY BE MOST USEFUL

- Anger Management/Aggression
- Bullying Perpetrator
- Parenting Skills/Discipline
- Self-Esteem Building
- Social Skills/Peer Relationships

SUGGESTIONS FOR USING THIS EXERCISE WITH STUDENT(S)

The "I" statement developed by Thomas Gordon is a method of self-expression that allows the student to communicate personal feelings without blaming or judging the other person or telling him or her what to do. Frequently, students communicate a point of view by using sentences that begin with "you" (e.g., you make me feel angry, you make me so jealous, you make me want to cry). These "you" statements can lead to antagonism, arguments, or angry reactions. "I" statements are a respectful method of expressing feelings while continuing to take responsibility for personal emotions.

Sometimes, students want to specify the change in behavior they are hoping to see. This can be done by indicating a wished-for change in behavior (e.g., I wish you would stop, I wish you would change that behavior). The wished- or hoped-for change should be stated after the "I" statement is given. It is used to clarify the feelings of the person delivering the "I" statement and is not directly telling the other person what to do.

Discuss the three components of the "I" statement with the student alone or in a group. Read the examples given in the activity and the explanation of the purpose of using "I" statements to express feelings. Ask the student to develop three "I" statements to address situations that are personally upsetting or frustrating; then instruct the student to formulate an "I" statement that communicates a positive feeling. The student may add "I wish you would . . ." to the end of the "I" statement if he or she wants to emphasize the problem. This activity is appropriate for students in grades 2 through 12.

SPEAKING SKILLS

"I" statements will help you communicate how you feel in a polite, respectful way that does not tell the other person what to do. They explain how you feel and let the other person decide how he or she can help to solve the problem. Because you haven't blamed or judged the other person or told him or her what to do, he or she is much more likely to want to change his or her behavior so that you will feel better. You can use "I" statements in many situations with most people that you know.

Not all people will respond to your "I" statements. Some have not learned to care about the way others feel, but it is always worth a try to see if someone whose behavior is bothering you is able to respect your feelings and avoid conflict. Try some "I" statements with your classmates, teachers, and family members. See how many times an "I" statement can solve a problem without any other action being necessary. If your "I" statements don't work with some people, ask your teacher or counselor for some other ideas of how to resolve the conflict.

"I" statements help us express facts and feelings by stating

1. How we feel . . .
2. When . . . and
3. Why . . .

I feel happy when all of my homework is done, because then I can have some fun.

I feel frustrated when I don't understand the lesson, because then I don't know how to do my assignments.

I feel unhappy when I have no one to play with, because I enjoy doing things with my friends.

Develop three "I" statements that would help you communicate a problem and one "I" statement to communicate a positive feeling to another person.

1. I feel _____

    when _____

    because _____

2. I feel _____

    when _____

    because _____

3. I feel _____

    when _____

    because _____

4. I feel _____

    when _____

    because _____

Sometimes, it is helpful to add, "I wish you would stop" or "I wish you would change your behavior." Try adding a wish or a hope to your "I" statements.

1. I feel _____

    when _____

    because _____

    I wish you would _____

2. I feel _____

    when _____

    because _____

    I wish you would _____

3. I feel _____

    when _____

    because _____

    I wish you would _____

4. I feel _____

    when _____

    because _____

    I wish you would _____

List several people you know with whom you will try an "I" statement during the following week.

_____   _____

_____   _____

_____   _____

_____   _____

PLANNING FOR FUN

GOALS OF THE EXERCISE

1. Participate in several organized or informal extracurricular activities per month.
2. Determine specific activities of personal interest.
3. Designate friends or groups to join in specified activities.
4. Develop a plan for participation in one specified activity.
5. Evaluate the plan after the activity is completed.

ADDITIONAL PROBLEMS FOR WHICH THIS EXERCISE MAY BE MOST USEFUL

- Divorce
- Grief/Loss
- Suicide Ideation/Attempt
- Social Skills/Peer Relationships

SUGGESTIONS FOR USING THIS EXERCISE WITH STUDENT(S)

Depressed students find it difficult to muster the motivation and energy required for participation in activities that are considered fun and enjoyable by their peers. These students lack the organizational and planning skills necessary for joining in even the most common extracurricular activities (e.g., attending a school sports event, play, fair, dance). Often, they will drop out of social gatherings and develop introverted habits that only contribute to their depressed condition.

The Planning for Fun activity is designed to encourage the student to engage in a leisure-time event by providing the step-by-step tools required to plan for a social outing with a friend or group of friends. Instruct the student to list some activities that he or she considers fun or that he or she enjoyed in the past. If the student has trouble completing this list, use the brainstorming method or suggest that he or she seek ideas from friends or parents. Indicate to the student that activities with others require some planning, and discuss the steps required to organize an activity with others. Assign the student to complete a plan for his or her chosen activity with others and to share the plan with you during a counseling session. After the activity has been completed, evaluate the plan and discuss any parts of it that will need revision during a subsequent counseling session. Gain a commitment from the student to try this process again with another event during the following week. The purpose of the activity is to support the student in taking a proactive approach in planning for social activities on a regular basis. This assignment is appropriate for students in grades 5 through 12.

PLANNING FOR FUN

Often, fun and leisure-time activities require some planning and organization. Think about the things you enjoy doing the most (e.g., reading; playing games or sports; watching movies; shopping; building; creating; doing mechanical activities). Activities that you do with others usually take more planning than those you do alone.

List some leisure-time activities you want to participate in during the next month. Designate school-related activities with the letter S, community activities with the letter C, activities that you will do with a friend or group with the letter F, and activities that you will participate in alone with the letter A.

_____   _____
_____   _____
_____   _____
_____   _____

Choose one of the activities that you would enjoy that requires the participation of one or several friends: _____

Planning an activity with others requires the following steps:

1. Decide which friend or friends you want to have join with you in the activity.
2. Discuss the activity with the friend or group of friends you have selected.
3. Ask the other(s) to participate.
4. Set a time and place for the activity.
5. Arrange for transportation and expenses and get permission from parents if necessary.
6. Make sure that all involved people agree to the plan.

Make the plans necessary for your chosen activity by completing the following checklist. Check each step after you complete it.

1. List the friends you would like to participate in this activity { }

_____   _____
_____   _____
_____   _____

2. Decide when and where you will talk to your friends about the activity and invite them to participate { }

    When and where will I talk to my friend(s): _____

    When and where will I talk to my friend(s): _____

3. Decide on a time and place for the activity { }

    Time: _____   Place: _____

4. Plan for all necessary conditions for successful participation in the activity
    *   Arrange for transportation { }

        Plan: _____

        _____

    *   Determine how to cover the costs { }

        Plan: _____

        _____

    *   Ask parents for permission { }

5. Get a verbal agreement from all to participate in the activity { }

    _____   _____

    _____   _____

After the activity is over, evaluate it to see how well your plan worked out.

Comments about the activity I planned: _____

_____

_____

Things I really liked about the activity:

_____   _____

_____   _____

Things about the plan or the activity that didn't work out:

_____   _____

_____   _____

Things I will do differently next time to create a better plan:

_____   _____

_____   _____

Additional comments:

_____

_____

_____

_____

The following week, an activity I would like to organize is

_____

_____

Remember, the more activities you plan and organize, the more activities you will be asked to participate in by others. This is a great way to make friends and enjoy your leisure time.

ACCOMPLISHMENTS I AM PROUD OF

GOALS OF THE EXERCISE

1. Affirm self for attaining personal goals and objectives.
2. Document personal accomplishments.
3. Improve efforts in various areas of personal functioning.
4. Enhance self-confidence and self-esteem.

ADDITIONAL PROBLEMS FOR WHICH THIS EXERCISE MAY BE MOST USEFUL

- Academic Motivation
- Self-Esteem Building
- Social Skills/Peer Relationships
- Suicide Ideation/Attempt

SUGGESTIONS FOR USING THIS EXERCISE WITH STUDENT(S)

Students who experience depression, anxiety, low self-esteem, and a lack of academic motivation tend to discount or completely overlook their personal accomplishments and goals or objectives that have been reached through personal effort. The Accomplishments I Am Proud Of assignment encourages students to record memorable events and accomplishments that trigger personal pride and recognition. Instruct the student to identify several goals and objectives that have been reached during his or her lifetime and to record the accomplishment by drawing a picture or pasting a photo that captures the moment of personal pride. This process will allow the student to affirm him- or herself for reaching goals in various areas of personal functioning.

The recognition of personal accomplishments should continue throughout the course of counseling, and additional accomplishments can be recorded by making as many copies of the activity pages as necessary. The assignment sheets should be entered in a personal journal kept by the student to document his or her progress in establishing healthy self-esteem and overcoming self-defeating methods of addressing problems and distress. Encourage the student to continue adding entries to the personal journal after his or her counseling has been terminated. This activity is appropriate for students in grades 3 through 12.

ACCOMPLISHMENTS I AM PROUD OF

Sometimes we forget to congratulate ourselves for our personal successes and accomplishments. We may experience positive feelings at the time but then discount or forget that point of pride as time passes and we become involved in other issues and events. Each time we reach a goal or accomplish an objective on the way toward a goal, we should take time to recognize and congratulate ourselves for our efforts. This affirmation will help us develop healthy self-confidence and self-esteem and greatly enhance our personal progress in the future.

Record some of your personal points of pride on the following lines by identifying a time when you reached a personal goal or objective. These accomplishments can be in any area of your life (e.g., academic, social, athletic, spiritual, creative, personal, work-related, family). After you have identified the accomplishment, draw a picture or paste a photograph that illustrates or captures the event. Keep this activity in a personal journal as an ongoing documentation of the many goals you achieve as you grow and mature. Make as many copies of the accomplishment-description pages as you need.

An Accomplishment I Am Proud Of (describe the accomplishment):

_____

_____

_____

_____

Draw or paste a picture of your accomplishment:

An Accomplishment I Am Proud Of (describe the accomplishment):

_____

_____

_____

_____

Draw or paste a picture of your accomplishment:

An Accomplishment I Am Proud Of (describe the accomplishment):

_____

_____

_____

_____

Draw or paste a picture of your accomplishment:

PROBLEM-SOLVING WORKSHEET

GOALS OF THE EXERCISE

1. Identify inappropriate personal behavior.
2. Increase awareness of the effect of misbehavior on self and others.
3. Develop cause-and-effect thinking.
4. Recognize appropriate solutions to behavioral problems.

ADDITIONAL PROBLEMS FOR WHICH THIS EXERCISE MAY BE MOST USEFUL

- Attention-Deficit/Hyperactivity Disorder (ADHD)
- Conflict Management
- Oppositional Defiant Disorder (ODD)
- Social Maladjustment/Conduct Disorder

SUGGESTIONS FOR USING THIS EXERCISE WITH STUDENT(S)

It is useful to involve the student in designing a consequence or remedy whenever his or her inappropriate behavior has created a problem. This process allows the student to recognize that violating the personal guidelines of *regard*, *respect*, and *responsibility* has a negative impact on both oneself and on others. The Problem-Solving Worksheet helps the student to begin this process by identifying the problem and relating the problem to a personal guideline. Next, the student is asked to recognize the effect of the action on him- or herself and on any other injured party. A plan for a consequence or remedy that will provide the student with a learning opportunity is requested, as is a list of appropriate behaviors that the student plans to use the next time a similar situation occurs. Students can be quite fair and appropriate when asked to examine their own behavior, and the consequence or remedy they suggest is often very effective for the following reasons:

- They become invested in the plan.
- They know what works best with them.
- They would rather design a consequence than have an adult do it for them.

If the student's plan is incomplete, inadequate, or inappropriate, the supervising adult (parent, teacher, or counselor) always reserves the right to substitute a different consequence or remedy.

INSTRUCTIONS FOR USING THE PROBLEM-SOLVING WORKSHEET

(These instructions can be discussed with, read to, or given to the student to read.)

Developing a plan to solve a problem that you have created can be a helpful method of learning from a mistake and figuring out a better way to deal with a similar situation next time. When students help determine an appropriate consequence or remedy for their own problem, the result is usually much more positive than when the teacher, parent, or other adult tries to figure out a solution without input from the students.

Find a quiet place where you can think about the problem without too many distractions. Then complete the entire worksheet, writing down as much information as possible about the situation you are trying to resolve. If you run out of room, use the back of the worksheet.

WHAT HAPPENED?

First, it is important to determine what happened. This means what was going on right before the problem occurred that may have contributed to the problem. What were you doing or saying? What were you thinking? What were others who were involved doing or saying? Write down anything that you think should be part of explaining what happened.

WHICH GUIDELINE DID I IGNORE?

The guidelines for appropriate behavior and social success include regard, respect, and responsibility for self and others. All behavior that causes problems is related to one of these guidelines.

Examples:

- *Jim hits Julie in the bus line. (regard)*
- *Jerry will not participate in his cooperative group. (responsibility)*
- *Susie tells false stories about Lisa. (respect)*
- *Jenny writes obscene words on the bathroom wall. (respect, responsibility)*
- *Josh calls the principal "Mr. Turkey." (respect)*
- *Danell throws food on the floor. (responsibility)*
- *Ellen teases or disses Tony. (respect)*

Determine which guideline you ignored when the problem occurred. Write it down in the space provided.

HOW DID MY BEHAVIOR CAUSE A PROBLEM FOR SOMEONE ELSE?

Inappropriate behavior usually causes a problem for others, such as your teacher, parent, classmates, or siblings. Who was directly affected in a negative way by your problem behavior? Write down the names of the affected people and how the behavior caused them difficulty.

HOW DID MY BEHAVIOR CAUSE A PROBLEM FOR ME?

All problem behavior eventually causes a problem for you. What kinds of consequences, hassles, struggles, or frustrations are you now dealing with as a result of your behavior or mistake? Write your ideas down in this section of the worksheet.

MY PLAN FOR A CONSEQUENCE OR REMEDY IS . . .

The best way to handle a mistake or problem is to think of a consequence that will ensure that the same behavior will not happen again and to fix any damage or hurt done to another person. Look at what you have written in the How Did My Behavior Cause a Problem for Someone Else? lines. Decide how you can make things right with the person or people who were affected. Then decide what will teach you a different and more appropriate way of behaving. Think of a consequence that will help you remember not to behave in ways that hurt you or someone else. The consequence should be powerful enough to help you change your behavior. Try to make the consequence fit the problem (e.g., if the problem occurred at recess, the consequence could be to miss several recesses and think about what happened, or if the problem involved hurting or disrespecting a classmate, the consequence could be to help that classmate in a way that builds a more positive relationship). You are the most important part of the consequence or remedy. Make sure to think of something that will make a real difference for you.

NEXT TIME I PLAN TO . . .

It's impossible to get rid of a negative behavior unless you have a positive behavior to replace it with. Possibly you already know what you wish you would have done instead of using an inappropriate behavior. Now is your chance to plan for what you want to do next time. Possibly you will use words instead of hitting or use respectful language to ask a question or make a comment. Think of as many positive ways as possible to deal with a similar situation. Write all of your ideas down and pick one or two to use next time. If you need help with this part, be sure to ask your parents, teachers, social worker, counselor, or other helpful classmates or adults.

When you have completed the worksheet, share it with the supervising adult who asked you to fill it out. He or she will want to discuss it with you to make sure that it is complete and has a good chance for success. It may take one or two attempts to come up with a plan that will work, but the positive results in developing regard, respect, and responsibility for oneself and others is well worth your time and effort. Good luck!

PROBLEM-SOLVING WORKSHEET

PERSONAL GUIDELINES

- Regard for self and others
- Respect for self and others
- Responsibility to self and others

What happened?

_____

_____

_____

Which guideline did I ignore?

_____

How did my behavior cause a problem for someone else?

_____

_____

_____

How did my behavior cause a problem for me?

_____

_____

_____

My plan for a consequence or remedy is . . .

_____

_____

_____

Next time, I plan to . . .

_____

_____

_____

Name: _____ Date: _____

Supervising Adult: _____

STUDENT SELF-REPORT

GOALS OF THE EXERCISE

1. Gain an awareness of appropriate emotional reactions, social interactions, and behavior.
2. Enhance ability to demonstrate self-control and make appropriate behavioral choices during various school activities and assignments.
3. Consider factors that contribute to or detract from appropriate behavior.
4. Measure and graph appropriate behavior over a specified period.

ADDITIONAL PROBLEMS FOR WHICH THIS EXERCISE MAY BE MOST USEFUL

- Academic Motivation
- Oppositional Defiant Disorder (ODD)
- Responsible Behavior Training
- Learning Difficulties
- Attention-Deficit/Hyperactivity Disorder (ADHD)

SUGGESTIONS FOR USING THIS EXERCISE WITH STUDENT(S)

Self-monitoring is a method of focusing the student's attention on personal actions and frequently results in a positive change in the behavior being monitored. The Student Self-Report directs the student to observe his or her personal behavior and record incidents of appropriate behavior or self-control during various classroom or school activities. The specified categories include listening to others, independent work, small- and large-group activities, and additional behaviors targeted for development or improvement. Assign the student to complete the student self-report as the day progresses. Each behavior should be recorded with a slash mark in the appropriate category. The recording should not be done by the teacher, as this would diminish the effect of self-monitoring on the student's ability to exhibit appropriate behavior and self-control. The teacher's role should be to guide the student in observing and reporting his or her personal behavior. Younger students will need more assistance with listing the activities to be monitored, but they should record their positive efforts themselves. This activity is appropriate for students in grades 3 through 12 and can be adapted for use with younger students.

STUDENT SELF-REPORT

Name: _____ **Grade:** _____
Teacher(s): _____
Dates of Report: from _____ **to** _____

Use this self-report to measure appropriate emotional reactions, social interactions, and behavior for one week by recording your positive actions throughout the school day. Put a slash mark on the line provided each time you catch yourself behaving appropriately. At the end of each day, add up the number of positive behaviors and color or shade in the graph up to the level of appropriate behaviors that you have recorded. On Friday, total up the number of positive behaviors for the entire week and record that number in the space provided on the graph. Answer the questions about factors that influence your choice of behaviors or actions, and sign the record once it is complete. Show the report to your teacher and ask him or her to sign it also. Save your weekly self-report charts to track your progress throughout the school year.

ACTIVITY OR TASK   **APPROPRIATE RESPONSES**

	Mon.	Tues.	Wed.	Thurs.	Fri.
With the teacher(s)	_____	_____	_____	_____	_____
With classmates	_____	_____	_____	_____	_____
With the principal	_____	_____	_____	_____	_____
Other school staff	_____	_____	_____	_____	_____
Other students	_____	_____	_____	_____	_____

Independent Work

(I worked independently without asking for help.)

_____   _____   _____   _____   _____

Small-Group Activity

(I cooperated with group members to complete the task.)

_____   _____   _____   _____   _____

Whole-Group Activity

(I listened to others and spoke only when it was my turn.)

_____   _____   _____   _____   _____

Other Behaviors I Am Working On

_____

_____

_____

_____

Add up the total number of positive behaviors for each day. Use a calculator or get assistance from your teacher if necessary. Record the numbers in the following spaces.

Mon.   **Tues.**   **Wed.**   **Thurs.**   **Fri.**

_____   _____   _____   _____   _____

Which day did you have the largest number of appropriate behaviors? _____

Which day did you have the least number of appropriate behaviors? _____

This week my behavior was _most_ appropriate when I _____

_____

This week I was _least_ appropriate when I _____

_____

Now add up your total number of appropriate behaviors for the week: _____

APPROPRIATE BEHAVIOR GRAPH

Record the number of your appropriate behaviors each day and for the total week on the following graph by coloring or shading in the rectangles.

Appropriate Behaviors	Mon.	Tues.	Wed.	Thurs.	Fri.	Weekly Total
180						
150						
120						
90						
60						
30						

Compared to last week, my behavior, social interactions, and emotional responses improved _____ or did not improve _____ by _____ (number or percent of positive or negative results).

If your score improved this week, give yourself a big pat on the back.

Student signature: _____ Date: _____

Teacher signature: _____

Teacher's comments: _____

_____

_____

SIMILAR YET DIFFERENT

GOALS OF THE EXERCISE

1. Recognize that all human beings have differences and similarities.
2. Verbalize the value of diversity in the school, the community, and the world.
3. Identify similarities and differences among people of various groups.
4. Develop acceptance and tolerance toward people with diverse characteristics.

ADDITIONAL PROBLEMS FOR WHICH THIS EXERCISE MAY BE MOST USEFUL

- Anger Management/Aggression
- Conflict Management
- Social Maladjustment/Conduct Disorder
- Social Skills/Peer Relationships

SUGGESTIONS FOR USING THIS EXERCISE WITH STUDENT(S)

This activity is designed to help students of all ages recognize and value the similarities and differences among people of the world, including people in their family, school, and community. Students often consider diversity an unfamiliar or negative factor that creates distance among people within their school or community. The Similar Yet Different exercise helps the student view diversity as a positive influence that adds variety, excitement, adventure, and challenge to an environment and provides an opportunity to learn and expand personal experiences and thinking.

Instruct the student to compare and contrast him- or herself to another person in the family, the classroom, the school, the community, and the world. This process will help develop the realization that there are as many similarities as there are differences among people throughout the world. Caution the student to use acceptance and tolerance while listing the similarities and differences between him- or herself and another person. After the student has completed the comparisons, brainstorm the advantages of differences and common characteristics among people and assign the student to record these positive factors on the worksheet. This activity can be used individually or in a group and is appropriate for students in grades kindergarten through 12.

SIMILAR YET DIFFERENT

In our world, each person is special and unique. No two people have exactly the same looks, interests, abilities, beliefs, fingerprints, or DNA. There are differences between males and females and among people of different ages, countries, cultures, religions, races, and ethnic groups. Yet despite all these differences, in many ways we are all very much the same. All human beings need air to breathe, water to drink, and food to eat. There are similarities and differences among the members of your family, classroom, school, and community. Choose a person from each group and list the similarities and differences between yourself and that person. Take care to stay positive. Remember that similarities help us form common bonds with others and relate easily to their ideas and customs. Diversity provides variety, excitement, adventure, challenge, and an opportunity to learn and expand our experiences and thinking. It also offers us freedom from boredom; think of how dull the world would be if everyone looked, acted, dressed, and performed exactly the same as everyone else. We should be thankful for and celebrate the numerous similarities and differences among all individuals throughout the world.

Choose someone in your family and list the ways you are similar to and different from that person. Name of the person: _____

Similarities

Differences

_____

_____

_____

_____

_____

_____

_____

Choose someone in your classroom and list the ways you are similar to and different from that person. Name of the person: _____

Similarities

Differences

_____

_____

_____

_____   _____
_____   _____
_____   _____
_____   _____

Choose someone in your school and list the ways you are similar to and different from that person. Name of the person: _____

Similarities   **Differences**

_____   _____
_____   _____
_____   _____
_____   _____
_____   _____
_____   _____

Choose someone in your community and list the ways you are similar to and different from that person. Name of the person: _____

Similarities   **Differences**

_____   _____
_____   _____
_____   _____
_____   _____
_____   _____
_____   _____

Choose someone who lives in a different country and list the ways you are similar to and different from that person. Name of the person: _____

Similarities   **Differences**

_____   _____
_____   _____
_____   _____
_____   _____
_____   _____
_____   _____

The best aspect of having things in common with other people is

_____

_____

_____

The best thing about knowing people who are different than me is

_____

_____

_____

MEDIA ASSESSMENT

GOALS OF THE EXERCISE

1. Recognize the influence that popular media has on the tolerance of diversity.
2. Rate popular media according to its portrayal of diverse populations.
3. Recognize subtle biases or stereotypes used by local and national media.
4. Maintain a commitment to acceptance and tolerance despite media influence.

ADDITIONAL PROBLEMS FOR WHICH THIS EXERCISE MAY BE MOST USEFUL

- Anger Management
- Conflict Management
- Social Maladjustment/Conduct Disorder
- Social Skills/Peer Relationships
- School Violence Perpetrator

SUGGESTIONS FOR USING THIS EXERCISE WITH STUDENT(S)

The Media Assessment activity allows the student to review local and national media and determine if there is a positive, a negative, or a neutral bias toward diversity. Ask the student to identify various forms of media, including TV, the Internet, radio, movies, videos, video games, CDs, magazines, and newspapers that influence the thinking and behavior of the student population. The student then evaluates selected media by using an informal rating scale to determine any subtle bias or stereotyping of particular cultural, racial, ethnic, religious, gender, or age groups. The student can then rate popular media to determine which is accepting and tolerant to issues of diversity and which is negatively biased toward tolerance of diversity. The activity can be completed individually by the student or as a group activity, or it can be used to survey students class- or schoolwide to determine student opinion of popular media and its attitude toward diversity issues. After the student completes the evaluation, instruct him or her to answer questions about how the media influences his or her personal behavior and what can be done to maintain a positive attitude toward diversity despite negative influences in the media. This activity is appropriate for students in grades 6 through 12.

MEDIA ASSESSMENT

Many of our ideas about customs, styles, clothes, and behavior are influenced by the media we listen to, read, and watch. Some areas of popular media include TV, the Internet, radio, movies, videos, video games, CDs, magazines, and newspapers.

Name specific areas of popular media that influence the way you think, behave, believe, and relate to others.

_____   _____
_____   _____
_____   _____
_____   _____
_____   _____

Interview some of your friends and list some of the media they listen to, read, watch, or play.

_____   _____
_____   _____
_____   _____
_____   _____
_____   _____
_____   _____
_____   _____

Now, rate some of the media you have listed on a tolerance-of-diversity scale developed to determine whether cultural, racial, religious, age, and gender diversity are promoted, damaged, or not addressed by the media consumed by students in our culture.

Choose a popular TV program watched by you and/or other students in your class or school.

Name of TV program: _____   Network: _____

Rate the program you have selected according to the tolerance-of-diversity criteria given in the following list.

1 = very much   2 = somewhat   3 = occasionally   4 = not much   5 = not at all

1. Features people from different racial or ethnic backgrounds   1 2 3 4 5
2. Portrays people from various age groups   1 2 3 4 5
3. Portrays ethnic minorities in leadership roles   1 2 3 4 5
4. Reflects a positive attitude toward various ethnic, religious, and
   cultural minorities   1 2 3 4 5
5. Describes males and females as equally effective   1 2 3 4 5
6. Avoids negative stereotyping of people from diverse cultures,
   races, religions, and other minority groups   1 2 3 4 5
7. Avoids body image bias   1 2 3 4 5
8. Avoids age bias   1 2 3 4 5
9. Shows positive interactions among people with diverse
   backgrounds   1 2 3 4 5
10. Reflects the culture, habits, and customs of various races,
    religions, cultures, and backgrounds   1 2 3 4 5

Total tolerance-of-diversity score (the lower the score,
the more tolerance shown): _____

Choose a popular video game played by you and/or other students in your class or school.

Name of video game: _____ Manufacturer: _____

Rate the video game you have selected according to the tolerance-of-diversity criteria in the following list.

1 = very much   2 = somewhat   3 = occasionally   4 = not much   5 = not at all

1. Features characters from different racial or ethnic backgrounds   1 2 3 4 5
2. Portrays characters from various age groups   1 2 3 4 5
3. Portrays ethnic minorities in leadership roles   1 2 3 4 5
4. Reflects a positive attitude toward various ethnic, religious, and
   cultural minorities   1 2 3 4 5
5. Portrays males and females as equally effective   1 2 3 4 5
6. Avoids negative stereotyping of characters from diverse
   cultures, races, religions, and other minority groups   1 2 3 4 5
7. Avoids body image bias   1 2 3 4 5
8. Avoids age bias   1 2 3 4 5

9. Shows positive interactions among characters with diverse backgrounds   1   2   3   4   5

10. Reflects the culture, habits, and customs of various religions, races, cultures, and backgrounds   1   2   3   4   5

Total tolerance-of-diversity score (the lower the score, the more tolerance shown): _____

Choose a magazine or newspaper read by you and/or other students in your class or school.

Name of magazine or newspaper: _____ Where published: _____

Rate the magazine or newspaper you have selected according to the tolerance-of-diversity criteria in the following list.

1 = very much   2 = somewhat   3 = occasionally   4 = not much   5 = not at all

1. Features people from different racial or ethnic backgrounds   1   2   3   4   5
2. Portrays people from various age groups   1   2   3   4   5
3. Portrays ethnic minorities in leadership roles   1   2   3   4   5
4. Reflects a positive attitude toward various ethnic, religious, and cultural minorities   1   2   3   4   5
5. Describes males and females as equally effective   1   2   3   4   5
6. Avoids negative stereotyping of people from diverse cultures, races, religions, and other minority groups   1   2   3   4   5
7. Avoids body image bias   1   2   3   4   5
8. Avoids age bias   1   2   3   4   5
9. Shows positive interactions among people with diverse backgrounds   1   2   3   4   5
10. Reflects the culture, habits, and customs of various races, religions, cultures, and backgrounds   1   2   3   4   5

Total tolerance-of-diversity score (the lower the score, the more tolerance shown): _____

Choose a movie or video watched by you and/or other students in your class or school.

Name of movie or video: _____ Producer or director: _____

Rate the movie or video you have selected according to the tolerance-of-diversity criteria in the following list.

1 = very much   2 = somewhat   3 = occasionally   4 = not much   5 = not at all

1. Features people from different racial or ethnic backgrounds   1   2   3   4   5
2. Portrays people from various age groups   1   2   3   4   5
3. Portrays ethnic minorities in leadership roles   1   2   3   4   5
4. Reflects a positive attitude toward various ethnic, religious, cultural minorities   1   2   3   4   5
5. Describes males and females as equally effective   1   2   3   4   5
6. Avoids negative stereotyping of people from diverse cultures, races, religions, and other minority groups   1   2   3   4   5
7. Avoids body image bias   1   2   3   4   5
8. Avoids age bias   1   2   3   4   5
9. Shows positive interactions among people with diverse backgrounds   1   2   3   4   5
10. Reflects the culture, habits, and customs of various races, religions, cultures, and backgrounds   1   2   3   4   5

Total tolerance-of-diversity score (the lower the score, the more tolerance shown): _____

Choose a radio program listened to by you and/or other students in your class or school.

Name of program: _____ Producing station: _____

Rate the radio program you have selected according to the tolerance-of-diversity criteria in the following list.

1 = very much   2 = somewhat   3 = occasionally   4 = not much   5 = not at all

1. Features people from different racial or ethnic backgrounds   1   2   3   4   5
2. Portrays people from various age groups   1   2   3   4   5
3. Portrays ethnic minorities in leadership roles   1   2   3   4   5
4. Reflects a positive attitude toward various ethnic, religious, and cultural minorities   1   2   3   4   5
5. Describes males and females as equally effective   1   2   3   4   5
6. Avoids negative stereotyping of people from diverse cultures, races, religions, and other minority groups   1   2   3   4   5
7. Avoids body image bias   1   2   3   4   5
8. Avoids age bias   1   2   3   4   5
9. Presents positive interactions among people with diverse backgrounds   1   2   3   4   5
10. Reflects the culture, habits, and customs of various races, religions, cultures, and backgrounds   1   2   3   4   5

Total tolerance-of-diversity score (the lower the score, the more tolerance shown): _____

Choose a CD or other musical format listened to by you and/or other students in your class or school.

Name of CD or other musical format: _____ Entertainer or group: _____

Rate the music you have selected according to the tolerance-of-diversity criteria in the following list.

1 = very much   2 = somewhat   3 = occasionally   4 = not much   5 = not at all

1. Features people from different racial or ethnic backgrounds	1 2 3 4 5
2. Portrays people from various age groups	1 2 3 4 5
3. Portrays ethnic minorities in leadership roles	1 2 3 4 5
4. Reflects a positive attitude toward various ethnic, religious, and cultural minorities	1 2 3 4 5
5. Describes males and females as equally effective	1 2 3 4 5
6. Avoids negative stereotyping of people from diverse cultures, races, religions, and other minority groups	1 2 3 4 5
7. Avoids body image bias	1 2 3 4 5
8. Avoids age bias	1 2 3 4 5
9. Presents positive interactions among people with diverse backgrounds	1 2 3 4 5
10. Reflects the culture, habits, and customs of various races, religions, cultures, and backgrounds	1 2 3 4 5

Total tolerance-of-diversity score (the lower the score, the more tolerance shown): _____

Based on this informal survey, the media that reflects the most tolerant approach to diversity is _____

The media that is least tolerant toward diversity is _____

Rate the media you have evaluated according to the tolerance and acceptance shown toward diversity. List the media from most to least tolerant.

1. _____
2. _____
3. _____
4. _____
5. _____
6. _____

What conclusions have you drawn from this assessment of popular media?

_____

_____

_____

_____

How much influence do you think popular media has on you and your fellow students?

_____

_____

_____

_____

Will you make any changes to prevent popular media from creating unwanted biases in your thinking, belief system, behavior, and relationships with others?

_____

_____

_____

_____

DIVERSITY SUPPORT SCALE

GOALS OF THE EXERCISE

1. Analyze the school's approach to issues of diversity.
2. Consider the many factors that constitute diversity in the school setting.
3. Determine if the school policy on diversity is adequate or needs changing.
4. View diversity as a positive factor that strengthens the school climate.

ADDITIONAL PROBLEMS FOR WHICH THIS EXERCISE MAY BE MOST USEFUL

- Anger Management
- Conflict Management
- Poverty/Economic Factors
- Social Maladjustment/Conduct Disorder
- Social Skills/Peer Relationships

SUGGESTIONS FOR USING THIS EXERCISE WITH STUDENT(S)

The Diversity Support Scale activity is a tool to assist the student in conducting an informal assessment of the school's support and acceptance of diversity forms (e.g., ethnicity, culture, physical or mental disablement, gender, age, family constellation, religion). Review with the student the value of a diverse student body and staff and ask for opinions about whether school policy supports a positive approach to diversity or not. Brainstorm with the student several areas where school policy promotes tolerance and acceptance of all students. Then instruct the student to complete the survey that asks him or her to rate the school in several important policy areas concerning diversity. If there are questions the student cannot answer, instruct him or her to gather more information by asking staff members who are familiar with the school's policy (e.g., teachers, counselors, social workers, administrators). When the student completes the survey, ask him or her to rate the school policy by scoring the responses according to the formula indicated on the survey. The score will indicate whether the school's policy is proactive and comprehensive, somewhat concerned and effective, or lacking in effectiveness by failing to properly address the issues of diversity. This activity can be done individually or in a group and is appropriate for students in grades 7 through 12.

DIVERSITY SUPPORT SCALE

Diversity is a fact of daily life. It occurs in every area of our existence. It is vital that schools support a positive, proactive policy toward promoting tolerance and valuing and celebrating diversity. If embraced as a positive characteristic, diversity can contribute to the character, strength, and effectiveness of a school district and its student body. However, when diversity is viewed as a problem or is ignored, it can create divisiveness and destructive reactions among the staff and the student body. Rate your school on the following scale to determine whether diversity issues are being dealt with in a positive, proactive manner, only partially dealt with, or ignored altogether.

1. Our school provides barrier-free access for all disabilities according to the specifications of the Individuals with Disabilities Education Act (IDEA).

   Yes _____ No _____ Partial provisions _____ Not sure _____

2. Our school provides equal resources and opportunities for boys' and girls' athletics.

   Yes _____ No _____ Partial provisions _____ Not sure _____

3. Our school sponsors an ongoing multicultural curriculum that addresses diversity issues at all grade levels.

   Yes _____ No _____ Partial provisions _____ Not sure _____

4. Our school has developed a harassment policy for staff and students that protects the confidentiality of the involved parties.

   Yes _____ No _____ Partial provisions _____ Not sure _____

5. Our school promotes appropriate sports-fan behavior, bans taunting, and encourages recognition of each team's efforts and abilities.

   Yes _____ No _____ Partial provisions _____ Not sure _____

6. Our school sponsors peer mediation, conflict management, and other programs to develop peacemaking skills and helps all students feel accepted and valued.

   Yes _____ No _____ Partial provisions _____ Not sure _____

7. Our school has established a policy that bans access to Internet sites and other media that promote hate, harassment, and pornographic materials.

   Yes _____ No _____ Partial provisions _____ Not sure _____

8. Our school bans any gang or divisive symbols on school property.

   Yes _____ No _____ Partial provisions _____ Not sure _____

9. Our school sponsors multicultural activities, clubs, and projects at all grade levels.

   Yes _____ No _____ Partial provisions _____ Not sure _____

10. Our school calendar respects religious diversity and the major holidays of all religious groups.

    Yes _____ No _____ Partial provisions _____ Not sure _____

11. Our school sponsors activities for people of all ages, including preschoolers, school-age children, adults, and senior citizens.

    Yes _____ No _____ Partial provisions _____ Not sure _____

12. Our school has an open employment policy that encourages the recruitment and hiring of people from diverse cultures, races, religions, gender, ages, and ethnic backgrounds.

    Yes _____ No _____ Partial provisions _____ Not sure _____

13. Our school values and celebrates diversity in all areas.

    Yes _____ No _____ Partial provisions _____ Not sure _____

Now create some additional criteria of your own for determining how your school addresses the issues of diversity.

1. _____

   _____

   Yes _____ No _____ Partial provisions _____ Not sure _____

2. _____

   _____

   Yes _____ No _____ Partial provisions _____ Not sure _____

3. _____

   _____

   Yes _____ No _____ Partial provisions _____ Not sure _____

4. _____

   _____

   Yes _____ No _____ Partial provisions _____ Not sure _____

5. _____

_____

Yes _____ No _____ Partial provisions _____ Not sure _____

Give your school a score for its policies regarding diversity. If you are not sure about a particular policy, check with your teacher, counselor, or school administrator to determine the school's policy on that issue.

5 = yes   3 = partial provisions   0 = no

Total score my school has earned in its overall diversity policy: _____

90 = a very conscientious diversity policy

75–90 = diversity issues are considered important

50–75 = some issues are addressed, but more work needs to be done in several areas

below 50 = diversity issues are not a priority and lack of tolerance may be a problem in several areas

What conclusions have you drawn from this assessment of your school's policies on diversity?

_____

_____

_____

Which areas need to be addressed by school policymakers, staff members, and student body?

_____

_____

_____

RESPECT AND TOLERANCE RATING INDEX

GOALS OF THE EXERCISE

1. Measure the tolerance level of self, family, and peer group.
2. Recognize the areas where tolerance and acceptance are demonstrated, as well as deficit areas.
3. Identify the many factors that contribute to tolerance.
4. Commit to renew efforts to enhance personal, family, and peer group tolerance.

ADDITIONAL PROBLEMS FOR WHICH THIS EXERCISE MAY BE MOST USEFUL

•Anger Management
•Conflict Management
•Social Maladjustment/Conduct Disorder
•Social Skills/Peer Relationships
•School Violence Perpetrator

SUGGESTIONS FOR USING THIS EXERCISE WITH STUDENT(S)

The Respect and Tolerance Rating Index is an informal method of measuring personal tolerance as well as the tolerance demonstrated by the student's family and peer group. The activity will familiarize the student with factors that contribute to regard, respect, and acceptance toward people of divergent groups. Completing the survey will help the student identify specific areas where tolerance is demonstrated and indicate deficit areas where tolerance is lacking. Ask the student to rate his or her personal attitude and behavior toward diversity first and then proceed to evaluate his or her family and peer group according to the same criteria. The student will be able to determine a diversity score for him- or herself and for his or her family and peer group by following the formula provided in the activity. Instruct the student to complete the activity by determining what further action needs to be made to improve the three tolerance ratings.

The activity can be done with the student individually but is probably more effective if done in a diversity, anger management, or conflict management group or in a classroom. The student can then compare his or her scores with other group members and discuss the implications of the tolerance scores with classmates. The group awareness of personal reactions to diversity, as well as the predicted reactions of family and peer group members, can inspire the student to commit to a more positive, proactive approach to promoting tolerance and celebrating diversity. This activity is appropriate for students in grades 7 through 12.

RESPECT AND TOLERANCE RATING INDEX

Personal, family, and peer group values, attitudes, and behavior are the key to acceptance and tolerance of diversity. The school or community may have excellent policies in place to promote an atmosphere of acceptance and tolerance; however, if personal actions are not consistent with such policies, no change in the level of respect, regard, and cooperation among diverse individuals or groups will occur. Appreciation of diversity begins with you. Check your personal attitude toward diversity first and then evaluate your family and peer group for their proactive approach to diversity.

MY PERSONAL LEVEL OF TOLERANCE AND APPRECIATION OF DIVERSITY

1. I am aware that I may have hidden biases and a tendency to stereotype others who are different, and I am working to examine and overcome these biases.

    Yes _____   Sometimes _____   No _____

2. I make an effort to treat all people with consideration and respect, regardless of their individual differences.

    Yes _____   Sometimes _____   No _____

3. I have ongoing friendships with people from a variety of backgrounds (e.g., different races, religions, cultures, gender, ages, physical abilities).

    Yes _____   Sometimes _____   No _____

4. I can accept corrective feedback about how my words and actions may negatively affect others from diverse groups.

    Yes _____   Sometimes _____   No _____

5. I speak up when I hear prejudicial remarks, jokes, or slurs or see behavior that is intolerant and disrespectful toward people from diverse groups.

    Yes _____   Sometimes _____   No _____

6. I participate in at least one diversity program at school or church or in the community.

    Yes _____   Sometimes _____   No _____

7. I believe that diversity is an asset that contributes strength and character to any group.

    Yes _____   Sometimes _____   No _____

8. I will work for tolerance and respect in my school and community for people of all abilities, beliefs, cultures, races, gender, and other diverse characteristics.

    Yes _____   Sometimes _____   No _____

MY FAMILY'S LEVEL OF TOLERANCE AND APPRECIATION OF DIVERSITY

1. My family members are aware of our hidden biases and tendencies to stereotype others who are different, and we are working to examine and overcome these biases.

    Yes _____   Sometimes _____   No _____

2. My family makes an effort to treat all people with consideration and respect, regardless of their individual differences.

    Yes _____   Sometimes _____   No _____

3. My family has ongoing friendships with people from a variety of backgrounds (e.g., races, religions, cultures, gender, ages, physical abilities).

    Yes _____   Sometimes _____   No _____

4. My family members can accept corrective feedback about how their words and actions may negatively affect others from diverse groups.

    Yes _____   Sometimes _____   No _____

5. My family members will speak up when they hear prejudicial remarks, jokes, or slurs or see behavior that is intolerant and disrespectful toward people from diverse groups.

    Yes _____   Sometimes _____   No _____

6. My family participates in at least one diversity program at school or church or in the community.

    Yes _____   Sometimes _____   No _____

7. My family believes that diversity is an asset that contributes strength and character to any group.

    Yes _____   Sometimes _____   No _____

8. My family is willing to work for tolerance and respect in our community for people of all abilities, beliefs, cultures, races, gender, and other diverse characteristics.

    Yes _____   Sometimes _____   No _____

MY PEER GROUP'S LEVEL OF TOLERANCE AND APPRECIATION OF DIVERSITY

1. My peer group is aware of its hidden biases and tendencies to stereotype others who are different, and we are working to examine and overcome these biases.

    Yes _____   Sometimes _____   No _____

2. My peer group makes an effort to treat all people with consideration and respect, regardless of their individual differences.

    Yes _____   Sometimes _____   No _____

3. My peer group has ongoing friendships with people from a variety of backgrounds (e.g., races, religions, cultures, gender, ages, physical abilities).

    Yes _____   Sometimes _____   No _____

4. My peer group members can accept corrective feedback about how their words and actions may negatively affect others from diverse groups.

    Yes _____   Sometimes _____   No _____

5. My peer group members will speak up when they hear prejudicial remarks, jokes, or slurs or see behavior that is intolerant and disrespectful toward people from diverse groups.

    Yes _____   Sometimes _____   No _____

6. My peer group participates in at least one diversity program at school or church or in the community.

    Yes _____   Sometimes _____   No _____

7. My family believes that diversity is an asset that contributes strength and character to any group.

    Yes _____   Sometimes _____   No _____

8. My peer group is willing to work for tolerance and respect in our school and community for people of all abilities, beliefs, cultures, races, gender, and other diverse characteristics.

    Yes _____   Sometimes _____   No _____

Now score your personal tolerance responses and those you have attributed to your family and peer group by using the following formula:

5 = yes   3 = sometimes   0 = no

My personal tolerance-of-diversity score: _____

My family's tolerance-of-diversity score: _____

My peer group's tolerance-of-diversity score: _____

How to evaluate these scores:

30–40 = A real concern for diversity issues—Keep up the good work!

20–30 = An awareness of the existence of diversity as an important issue—Pledge to do more to make a difference!

0–20 = A lack of awareness that tolerance of diversity matters—Time to get educated on this important issue!

Based on my informal assessment of attitudes toward diversity,

Ways that I can improve my personal approach to tolerance and diversity awareness include:

_____
_____
_____
_____

Ways that my family can improve its approach to tolerance and diversity awareness include:

_____
_____
_____
_____

Ways that my peer group can improve its approach to tolerance and diversity awareness include:

_____
_____
_____
_____

IMPORTANT PEOPLE IN MY LIFE

GOALS OF THE EXERCISE

1. Develop an awareness of the need for others.
2. Recognize the existing support system.
3. View family, friends, and teachers as positive, loving, and helpful.
4. Strengthen relationships with significant others.
5. Enhance feelings of support and security.

ADDITIONAL PROBLEMS FOR WHICH THIS EXERCISE MAY BE MOST USEFUL

- Blended Family
- Depression
- Grief/Loss
- Self-Esteem Building
- Social Skills/Peer Relationships

SUGGESTIONS FOR USING THIS EXERCISE WITH STUDENT(S)

Students dealing with family disruption, depression, or grief and loss often believe that no one loves or cares for them. Feelings of isolation may develop that are based on false or skewed assumptions. Recognition of a personal support system enhances self-esteem and reduces anxiety and feelings of helplessness and hopelessness. This exercise helps the student to increase awareness of those people in his or her life who do care about and are willing to help with his or her personal concerns. The student will then discover the positive nature of relationships within the immediate and extended family and begin to view family members and other caring people from a more positive perspective. Ask the student to list family members, relatives, friends, mentors, and role models who offer special support, encouragement, and unconditional love. When the list is complete, the student may draw a picture of him- or herself with one of the listed significant others. Eight additional suggestions for activities involving supportive others in the student's life are listed following the Important People in My Life activity. This exercise is appropriate for students in grades kindergarten through 12. For younger students, the counselor can assist in writing the names and describing the meaning of significant others in more detail.

INTRODUCTION TO THE STUDENT

Identify several positive people in your life by writing their names on the lines provided under the categories of family, relatives, friends, and so on. Fill in each line and, if necessary, brainstorm examples of additional caring people in your life with your parents, counselor, teacher, or a friend.

- *Family* is the group of close, immediate relatives whom you live with, including your parents and siblings.
- *Relatives* are extended family members, including grandparents, aunts, uncles, and cousins.
- *Mentors* are those special teachers, coaches, or counselors who have helped you learn important lessons.
- *Role models* are people you admire and would like to identify with or emulate.

This list can be added to as your counseling progresses and your awareness of your personal support system increases. An optional activity is to select one special supportive person from your list and draw a picture of yourself with this person. Be sure to show the nature of the caring relationship in the picture and to discuss your ideas and feelings with your counselor during the next session.

IMPORTANT PEOPLE IN MY LIFE

Create a network of special people who contribute to your healthy self-esteem. Add more lines if necessary.

Family

_____   _____
_____   _____
_____   _____

Relatives

_____   _____
_____   _____
_____   _____

Friends

_____   _____
_____   _____
_____   _____

Teachers and Mentors

_____   _____
_____   _____
_____   _____

Role Models

_____   _____
_____   _____
_____   _____

ADDITIONAL ACTIVITIES

1. This is a picture of my family (draw a picture of each person in your immediate family involved in an activity, name each person, and describe the activity):

2. Relatively speaking (write a story and/or draw a picture describing your relatives):

3. Important friendships (write a story and/or draw a picture of yourself and one or more of your friends):

4. Special teachers or mentors (write a story and/or draw a picture illustrating how a teacher or a mentor has helped you):

5. Role models in my life (write a story and/or draw a picture describing one of your role models):

6. A word about my parents (write a paragraph or story about your parents and draw a picture to illustrate the story):

7. List some ways your significant others show they care for you (write a paragraph or draw a picture to illustrate):

8. List some ways you show your significant others how important they are in your life (write a story and/or draw a picture to illustrate):

POSITIVE AND NEGATIVE CONSEQUENCES

GOALS OF THE EXERCISE

1. Understand the theory of cause and effect.
2. Recognize that consequences occur as a direct result of personal behavior.
3. Verbalize a sense of control over positive and negative consequences.
4. Agree to enhance personal efforts to create positive consequences for self and others.

ADDITIONAL PROBLEMS FOR WHICH THIS EXERCISE MAY BE MOST USEFUL

- Blended Family
- Depression
- Grief/Loss
- Self-Esteem Building
- Social Skills/Peer Relationships

SUGGESTIONS FOR USING THIS EXERCISE WITH STUDENT(S)

Students dealing with family disruption, depression, or low self-esteem often feel that they have little control over the events and outcomes in their lives. The Positive and Negative Consequences activity teaches the student about the law of cause and effect, which states that all behavior creates a result or an effect. Use this activity to help the student recognize that positive personal efforts create positive personal consequences and negative personal efforts create negative personal consequences. This will give the student a sense of empowerment and motivation to influence his or her personal world through positive choices and decisions.

Ask the student to read the introduction to the activity, which explains cause-and-effect theory. Discuss this information with the student and instruct him or her to apply it to personal behaviors that have created either positive or negative consequences. The activity asks the student to list several scenarios and draw a picture of one situation that illustrates the theory. The same instructions are repeated for a negative behavior or decision. Finally, the student is asked to identify several pending situations in which a positive personal decision or behavior will determine a positive consequence for the student and his or her family, friends, or community. This activity is appropriate for students in grades 4 through 12 and can be adapted for use with younger students.

POSITIVE AND NEGATIVE CONSEQUENCES

Consequences happen as a direct result of our personal decisions and behavior. Appropriate, thoughtful, and cooperative behavior creates positive consequences; inappropriate, careless, hurtful, and uncooperative behavior creates negative consequences. We can control the consequences that occur in our life simply by controlling our behavior. For example, friendly and helpful behavior will result in friendships and popularity, whereas unfriendly and inconsiderate behavior results in peer problems and social isolation. Studying for a test will greatly improve your chances of getting a good grade, whereas neglecting to study will probably result in a poor grade. Doing your chores creates a positive relationship with your parents and the freedom to do the things you like, whereas neglecting your chores may result in your privileges being taken away until you complete the chores. Working hard to develop a musical, athletic, academic, or artistic ability will result in accomplishment, whereas not practicing or working will result in the talent or skill remaining undeveloped. This is called the *law of cause and effect*, which means that your positive efforts will cause positive results and your negative efforts will cause negative results. As it operates throughout your lifetime, this law will allow you to have great control over many events and consequences that you experience.

Think of several times when your positive efforts resulted in a positive consequence for you and/or others.

Positive Effort

_____

_____

_____

_____

Positive Result

_____

_____

_____

_____

Draw a picture or write a paragraph about a positive decision that resulted in a positive consequence for you.

Think of several times when your negative efforts resulted in a negative consequence for you and/or others.

Negative Effort   **Negative Result**

_____   _____

_____   _____

_____   _____

_____   _____

Draw a picture or write a paragraph about a negative decision that resulted in a negative consequence for you.

```




```

Now think about some current situations in which a positive choice or behavior could create a positive result. The best possible decisions are those that result in positive consequences for you and your family, friends, school, and community. List some personal positive efforts and predict the positive result.

Positive Effort   **Potential Positive Result**

_____   _____

_____   _____

_____   _____

_____   _____

MY EVOLVING FEELINGS ABOUT CHANGE, LOSS, AND GRIEF

GOALS OF THE EXERCISE

1. View grief as a process that evolves through several stages.
2. Differentiate between minor and significant losses.
3. Recognize which stage of grief and loss is being experienced.
4. View potential recovery from grief in optimistic terms.

ADDITIONAL PROBLEMS FOR WHICH THIS EXERCISE MAY BE MOST USEFUL

- Anxiety Reduction
- Attachment/Bonding Deficits
- Blended Family
- Depression
- Divorce

SUGGESTIONS FOR USING THIS EXERCISE WITH STUDENT(S)

Change and loss will affect the student numerous times during the course of his or her lifetime. Grief is the reaction felt as a result of being confronted by a change or loss. The feelings associated with grief will be experienced in varying degrees, depending on the significance of the change or loss on the student's life. The student will benefit from understanding grief as a process that evolves as he or she confronts, accepts, and finally adjusts to the loss. Some losses will create only minor frustration and irritation, whereas more significant losses will create feelings of devastation, anger, sadness, helplessness, and fear. The My Evolving Feelings About Change, Loss, and Grief activity will help the student develop his or her personal definition of grief and describe the personal feelings linked to the various stages of the grieving process. The activity asks the student to record feelings already experienced and to predict how those feelings will change as time passes and acceptance and adjustment occur. Finally, the student is instructed to record a positive memory related to his or her life prior to the loss by drawing a picture or pasting a photo on the activity sheet. The exercise is designed to give the student hope and optimism for the future while he or she continues to value the positive memories of the past. This activity is appropriate for students in grades 4 through 12 and can be used with younger students with the counselor's assistance.

MY EVOLVING FEELINGS ABOUT CHANGE, LOSS, AND GRIEF

Grief is often defined as our personal reaction to a change or loss. Each little change in our lives means that we experience some discomfort and frustration. As we begin to accept what has happened, our feelings adjust and we learn to live with the change and feel better about the change that the loss created. When a significant change or loss occurs (e.g., divorce, death, serious injury, illness), the feelings we experience are much stronger, and the time it takes to recover is longer, but the process is the same. At first, we feel devastated, sad, angry, and powerless, but slowly we adjust to the change so that our feelings become less painful and more optimistic. Eventually we are able to enjoy our lives again and experience happy, enthusiastic feelings. However, the significant loss will always remain in our memories as a bittersweet reminder of that time in our lives after which nothing would ever be the same.

If you have just experienced a significant loss, complete only as much of this activity as is appropriate. If the loss occurred a few weeks or months ago, skip question 4 and go on to questions 5 through 7. After you complete the questions, draw a picture or paste a photo of a pleasant experience in your life from before the loss.

1. Some people say that each change in our life creates grief or a feeling of loss. For me, grief means

   _____

   _____

   _____

   _____

2. When I first learned about the loss, I felt

   _____

   _____

   _____

   _____

3. A few weeks later, I felt

_____

_____

_____

_____

4. After several months, I felt

_____

_____

_____

_____

5. Now, after _____ (weeks, months, or years), I feel

_____

_____

_____

_____

6. Five years from now, I think I will feel

_____

_____

_____

_____

7. But I will always remember

_____

_____

_____

_____

8. Draw a picture or paste a photo of a pleasant experience in your life that occurred before the loss.

9. Describe what is happening in the picture or photo.

    _____

    _____

    _____

    _____

CLIMB THE MOUNTAIN

GOALS OF THE EXERCISE

1. Recognize that the grieving process takes time, energy, and effort.
2. Identify the several stages of the grieving process.
3. Identify feelings experienced during the different stages of grieving.
4. Recognize personal progress in working through grief.

ADDITIONAL PROBLEMS FOR WHICH THIS EXERCISE MAY BE MOST USEFUL

- Anxiety Reduction
- Attachment/Bonding Deficits
- Blended Family
- Depression
- Divorce

SUGGESTIONS FOR USING THIS EXERCISE WITH STUDENT(S)

The grieving process is painful and discouraging, especially when it seems like there is no end in sight. The Climb the Mountain activity helps the student to envision his or her personal grieving as a journey that progresses through several stages and ends in him or her adjusting to an altered life pattern and acquiring the ability to move ahead with optimism and enthusiasm. Ask the student to read the description of the several stages of grieving and record his or her personal time frame for each stage on the Grief Mountain drawing. Then instruct the student to describe in writing on the activity sheet his or her personal feelings and circumstances associated with each stage.

The exercise points out that grieving is much like climbing a mountain, in that it takes time, effort, and energy. It is impossible to rush the process or move on with life without first reaching each plateau and experiencing the thoughts and feelings unique to each stage. The activity is designed to give the student a sense of hope and empowerment in coping with a life-altering loss. As he or she tracks and records personal progress, a sense of courage and determination will emerge to motivate him or her to climb the mountain of grief and reach the ultimate goal of acceptance and adjustment. This activity is appropriate for students in grades 4 through 12 and can be used with younger students with additional assistance from the counselor.

CLIMB THE MOUNTAIN

Grief is your natural reaction to a loss in your life. If the loss is significant, creating major changes in your life, the grief process will take up most of your time, energy, and efforts for a substantial period. Living with grief is similar to climbing a mountain: Each challenging step brings you closer to the top, where you will reach the goal of overcoming grief and creating a happier life. But it is impossible to reach the top of the mountain without passing through each stage of the grieving process. The steps of grieving include the following:

1. Experiencing severe pain, shock, loss, and disbelief when the loss occurs
2. Acknowledging the loss gradually as you realize its effect on your feelings and your life
3. Experiencing feelings of sadness, anger, fear, anxiety, and helplessness
4. Adjusting to and living with the significant changes created by the loss
5. Moving on and investing in a happy life

Use Grief Mountain to track your progress through the grieving process. Draw a mountain by connecting the dots from top to bottom; then record the dates when you experienced each stage of grief on the lines provided. Write down some of your experiences and feelings as you progress toward the top of the mountain and your goal of living a happy life despite the sad events that occur. Remember that the secret to happiness is not to avoid painful experiences but, rather, to be able to cope with painful experiences when they happen. No one can prevent sad things from happening, but each of us can manage our grief so that we can regain our feelings of optimism and happiness.

Describe each stage of grief as you have experienced it:

1. Experiencing severe pain, shock, and disbelief when the loss occurs. During this time, my initial reaction to the loss is or was

_____

_____

_____

_____

_____

2. Acknowledging the loss gradually as I realize its effect on my feelings and my life. During this time, my reaction to the loss is or was

    _____

    _____

    _____

    _____

    _____

    _____

3. Experiencing feelings of sadness, anger, fear, anxiety, and helplessness. During this time, my reaction to the loss is or was

    _____

    _____

    _____

    _____

    _____

    _____

    _____

    _____

4. Adjusting to and living with the significant changes created by the loss. During this time, my reaction to the loss is or was

    _____

    _____

    _____

    _____

    _____

    _____

    _____

5. Moving on and investing in a happy life. During this time, I am feeling and experiencing

    _____

    _____

    _____

    _____

    _____

_____

_____

_____

6.   I will know that I am reaching the top of the mountain when I start to feel

_____

_____

_____

_____

_____

_____

_____

_____

CLIMB THE MOUNTAIN

Connect the dots to draw a picture of Grief Mountain. Then begin to climb, passing through all five stages of recovering from grief.

Moving on;
investing in
a happy life
_____

•

•

Adjusting to
the significant
change
_____

•

•

•

Experiencing
grief and pain •
_____

Acknowledging
the loss
•
_____

Disbelief;
severe pain •
_____

•

•

• Loss; shock;
numbness
of feeling
_____

BASE CAMP

GRIEF MOUNTAIN

EBB AND FLOW

GOALS OF THE EXERCISE

1. Recognize that ups and downs are a normal part of the flow of life.
2. Construct a personal and family history of significant events that have occurred.
3. Identify significant events that have contributed to personal and family joy and grief.
4. Predict future challenges and positive events likely to occur.

ADDITIONAL PROBLEMS FOR WHICH THIS EXERCISE MAY BE MOST USEFUL

- Anxiety Reduction
- Attachment/Bonding Deficits
- Blended Family
- Depression
- Divorce

SUGGESTIONS FOR USING THIS EXERCISE WITH STUDENT(S)

Life is an ongoing process of ebbs and flows, celebrations and sad events, unions and separations, births and deaths. The activity asks the student to create a timeline of his or her family's significant events, starting at least 10 years before his or her birth and continuing to the present. Suggestions for significant events are listed, and the student may add some additional events to fit his or her personal scenario. This exercise will help the student recognize that losses, along with positive circumstances, are a normal part of life. The student will also understand that his or her family has dealt with numerous ups and downs before and after his or her birth and that this process will continue into the future.

Discuss the personal and family timeline with the student; then have him or her select one positive and one negative event to describe in further detail. After consideration of past and current situations, instruct the student to predict what positive and challenging scenarios are likely to occur for him or her and his or her family in the future. The student should record these predictions sequentially to illustrate that the ebb and flow process is ongoing. This activity is appropriate for students in grades 3 through 12.

EBB AND FLOW

Life is an ongoing process of ebbs and flows, celebrations and sad events, unions and separations, births and deaths. Create a timeline of your family's significant events, starting at least 10 years before you were born and continuing to the present.

Some examples of significant events or family ebbs and flows include the following:

Aunt dies	My birthday	Stepsister is born
Brother moves out	Parent becomes ill	Uncle dies
Brother is born	Parent dies	Father/Mother getting promoted
Cousin is born	Parent remarries	
Family member becomes seriously ill	Parents divorce	Father/Mother losing job
	Parents marry	_____
Family move	Parents meet	_____
Family trip	Parents separate	_____
Grandfather dies	Sister moves out	_____
Grandmother dies	Sister is born	_____
Great-grandfather dies	Stepbrother is born	_____
Great-grandmother dies		_____

Add some additional significant events experienced by you or your family on the blank lines provided in the preceding list. Use the following ebb and flow chart to record some happy and sad events in your personal or family history. Record the event and the date when it happened. Use the ebb lines to record positive, happy events and the flow lines to record negative or sad events. Try to record the events in sequence or in the order they occurred.

THE EBB AND FLOW OF MY PERSONAL AND FAMILY LIFE

Ebb: Ebb: Ebb:

_____   _____   _____

Flow: Flow: Flow
_____   _____   _____

Ebb: Ebb: Ebb:
_____   _____   _____

Flow: Flow: Flow
_____   _____   _____

Write about an event that created joy and happiness for you and/or your family.

_____

_____

_____

_____

_____

Write about an event that created grief and sadness for you and/or your family.

_____

_____

_____

_____

_____

Your future life will contain a mixture of joyful and sad experiences. Some of these experiences may include the following:

High school graduation	Moving away from home	Leaving friends
College graduation	Losing a loved one	Reunions
Getting a job	Financial success	Personal illnesses
Getting married	Financial downturn	Buying a house
Having children	Children leaving home	_____
Having a mortgage	Retirement	_____
Children growing up	Getting older	_____

Predict some of the ups and downs you may experience as you continue to mature, change, and progress through life. Add some additional circumstances on the blank lines in the preceding list. Write some of the situations that may occur on the following spaces. Use the up lines for positive experiences and the down lines for challenging situations you may face in the future.

Up: _____

Up: _____

Up: _____

Down: _____

Down: _____

Down: _____

Up: _____

Up: _____

Up: _____

Down: _____

Down: _____

Down: _____

PERSONAL PROBLEM-SOLVING WORKSHEET

GOALS OF THE EXERCISE

1. Define a problem to be resolved.
2. Identify people needed to resolve the problem.
3. Brainstorm potential solutions to the problem.
4. Choose a strategy to solve the problem and record the results.

ADDITIONAL PROBLEMS FOR WHICH THIS EXERCISE MAY BE MOST USEFUL

- Attachment/Bonding Deficits
- Parenting Skills/Discipline
- Physical Disabilities/Challenges
- Responsible Behavior Training
- Suicide Ideation/Attempt

SUGGESTIONS FOR USING THIS EXERCISE WITH STUDENT(S)

Students often feel inadequate or unprepared to solve problems on their own and lack knowledge of how to effectively implement a step-by-step process for attaining strategies with positive results. The Personal Problem-Solving Worksheet assists the student in solving a problem by planning for a successful outcome. The student is asked to list the people needed to help resolve the problem and then to brainstorm strategies and to consider and list the possible results of each strategy. The student is instructed to select the strategy to be tried first and to choose a backup strategy in case the selected strategy does not work. Finally, the student is directed to record the result of the first strategy tried.

Use this activity with the student each time he or she expresses a concern about a problem. The worksheet can be completed by the student alone or with help during a counseling session. Instruct the student to keep the worksheets in a personal journal as a record of problems that have been solved and those that are in progress. The worksheets will affirm and reinforce the student's developing problem-solving abilities and offer encouragement when the student faces personal problems in the future. This activity can be used with students of all grade levels.

PERSONAL PROBLEM-SOLVING WORKSHEET

Use this sheet to plan a solution to a personal problem. Start by defining the problem and determining whether you can solve it alone or with help. List all of the people needed to help you. Think of several strategies to deal with the problem. Brainstorm possible solutions with your counselor, teacher, parent, or friends if you need additional ideas. Consider how each strategy might work out and select the one you want to try first. Choose a second strategy as a backup plan in case the first strategy doesn't work out as well as you had hoped. After you have given the strategy time to work, record the results and indicate whether the problem was solved. Keep your worksheets in a personal journal as a record of your problem-solving attempts and successes.

Problem: _____

_____

_____

_____

People needed to help me solve the problem:

_____   _____

_____   _____

_____   _____

Potential solutions:

Strategy   **Possible Outcome**

_____   _____

_____   _____

_____   _____

_____   _____

Strategy   **Possible Outcome**

_____   _____

_____   _____

_____   _____

_____   _____

The strategy I will try first: _____

_____

_____

_____

If that strategy doesn't work, I will: _____

_____

_____

_____

Result: _____

_____

_____

_____

What I will do next time a similar problem occurs: _____

_____

_____

_____

Name: _____

Date: _____

DECISION MAKING

GOALS OF THE EXERCISE

1. Develop positive decision-making skills.
2. Recognize that positive decisions result in positive consequences.
3. Consider poor decisions as learning opportunities.
4. Plan for several positive decisions in the near future.

ADDITIONAL PROBLEMS FOR WHICH THIS EXERCISE MAY BE MOST USEFUL

- Attention-Seeking Behavior
- Career Planning
- Divorce
- School Refusal/Phobia
- Sexual Responsibility

SUGGESTIONS FOR USING THIS EXERCISE WITH STUDENT(S)

Students are generally happy when they make positive or appropriate choices and upset and frustrated when they make poor decisions. The Decision-Making activity teaches the student to consider poor choices and mistakes as learning opportunities that can help him or her choose more wisely in the future. The activity asks the student to list several decisions he or she will make in the near future and to predict the negative result of making a poor choice and the positive result of making an appropriate choice. The exercise is designed to give the student a sense of control over the consequences that occur and to teach cause-and-effect thinking. The student is instructed to write how positive and negative choices make him or her feel and to state the advantages of making appropriate decisions. This activity should be followed up with a counseling session to review the choice statements made by the student and to further reinforce the concept that all decisions create an opportunity for attaining wisdom. This activity is appropriate for students in grades 4 through 12 and for younger students with additional assistance from the counselor.

DECISION MAKING

Both good and bad decisions can have a positive influence on your ability to problem-solve and make appropriate decisions in the future. Good decisions help you feel capable and confident; poor decisions help you learn to choose more wisely next time. Good decisions create positive consequences; poor decisions, negative consequences. Think of some decisions you will have to make in the next week. List these opportunities for decision making on the lines provided.

Situations that will give me the opportunity to make a choice:

_____   _____
_____   _____
_____   _____
_____   _____

Choose four opportunities for decision making and predict the consequences if you make a good choice.

Good Decisions I Will Try to Make   **Possible Consequences**

_____   _____
_____   _____
_____   _____
_____   _____

Now predict the consequences if you make a poor choice.

Poor Decisions I Will Try to Avoid   **Possible Consequences**

_____   _____
_____   _____
_____   _____
_____   _____

When I make a good choice, I feel _____

When I make a poor choice, I feel _____

The advantage of making a good choice is _____

_____

CHORE REPORT CARD

GOALS OF THE EXERCISE

1. Increase time and effort spent on chore completion.
2. Compare personal assessment of work quality with the assessment of parents.
3. Improve willingness to comply with parents' requests to complete chores.
4. Measure and graph chore completion over a specified period.

ADDITIONAL PROBLEMS FOR WHICH THIS EXERCISE MAY BE MOST USEFUL

- Academic Motivation
- Attention-Deficit/Hyperactivity Disorder (ADHD)
- Career Planning
- Learning Difficulties
- Responsible Behavior Training

SUGGESTIONS FOR USING THIS EXERCISE WITH STUDENT(S)

Self-monitoring is a method of focusing the student's attention on personal actions and frequently results in a positive change in the behavior being monitored. Students with ODD or ADHD or who lack responsibility and maturity tend to resist and procrastinate completing chores. The Chore Report Card directs the student to evaluate his or her weekly efforts to complete chores by assigning a grade for each effort and comparing these grades to those given by the parents. A list of typical chores is provided, as well as additional blank spaces for the student to record any additional chores that have been omitted.

Assign the student to fill out the Chore Report Card daily and then request his or her parents' input. The student is instructed to graph the number of chores completed at the end of each day and to calculate and graph the total number of chores completed at the week's end. Both the parents and the student are requested to sign the report card and to make any comments regarding the tasks completed that week and the attitude and effort evidenced by the student. Discuss the Chore Report Card with the student during the counseling session, giving encouragement for improvement shown and guidance in areas where progress is lacking. This activity is appropriate for students in grades 3 through 12; if used with younger children, it will require modification or additional assistance from the parents and counselor.

CHORE REPORT CARD

Name: _____   **Age:** _____

Dates of report: from _____   **to** _____

Use this report card to grade your efforts and success in completing your daily and weekly chores. Select the chores you are assigned from the list provided or add any other chores that you do daily or weekly. Write the name of the chore in the Job, Chore, or Task column; then give yourself a grade that measures the time and effort you invested in the S (for student) column under the day of the week in which the chore was completed. Ask your parents to give you a grade as well and to record this grade beside the grade you have given yourself in the column marked P (for parent). Use the weekly chore graph to monitor your daily and weekly rate of chore completion. Compare the current week's efforts with the previous week's accomplishments. Be sure to congratulate yourself for any improvement in your efforts.

Chores you may be asked to complete (add some of your own in the spaces provided):

Answer phone	Get ready for school	Take out the trash
Baby-sit	Grocery-shop	Vacuum
Clean room	Hang up coat	Wash car
Clean sink, tub, and toilet	Load dishwasher	Wipe kitchen counter
Clear table	Make lunch	_____
Collect dirty clothes	Make breakfast	_____
Do homework	Mop floor	_____
Do laundry	Mow lawn	_____
Dust	Pick up bathroom	_____
Feed pet(s)	Pick up toys or belongings	_____
Fold laundry	Run errands	_____
Garden	Set table	_____
Get dressed	Shovel walks	_____
Get ready for bed	Start dinner	_____

_____   _____   _____
_____   _____   _____
_____   _____   _____

JOB, CHORE, OR TASK   GRADES FOR EFFORT AND COMPLETION

	Mon.		Tues.		Wed.	
	S	P	S	P	S	P
_____	___	___	___	___	___	___
_____	___	___	___	___	___	___
_____	___	___	___	___	___	___
_____	___	___	___	___	___	___
_____	___	___	___	___	___	___
_____	___	___	___	___	___	___
_____	___	___	___	___	___	___

	Thurs.		Fri.		Sat.		Sun.	
	S	P	S	P	S	P	S	P
_____	___	___	___	___	___	___	___	___
_____	___	___	___	___	___	___	___	___
_____	___	___	___	___	___	___	___	___
_____	___	___	___	___	___	___	___	___
_____	___	___	___	___	___	___	___	___
_____	___	___	___	___	___	___	___	___
_____	___	___	___	___	___	___	___	___
_____	___	___	___	___	___	___	___	___

WEEKLY CHORE GRAPH

Record the number of chores you have completed each day and for the total week on the following graph by shading or coloring in the rectangles.

Chores Completed									
12									60 or more
10									50
8									40
6									30
3									20
2									10
0									0
	Mon.	Tues.	Wed.	Thurs.	Fri.	Sat.	Sun.	Weekly Total	

Parent's comments: _____

_____

Compared to last week my time and effort in completing chores improved _____ or did not improve _____ by _____ (number or percentage of positive or negative results). If your score improved this week, give yourself a big pat on the back.

Student's signature: _____ Date: _____
Student's comments: _____

_____

Parent's signature: _____ Date: _____
Parent's comments: _____

_____

RESPONSES TO CRITICISM, PRAISE, AND ENCOURAGEMENT

GOALS OF THE EXERCISE

1. Identify possible responses to praise, criticism, and encouragement.
2. Recognize personal feelings associated with criticism, praise, and encouragement.
3. Determine proactive methods to discourage criticism.
4. Maintain an independent and positive attitude toward self and personal efforts.

ADDITIONAL PROBLEMS FOR WHICH THIS EXERCISE MAY BE MOST USEFUL

- Academic Motivation
- Anger Management
- Attention-Seeking Behavior
- Learning Difficulties
- Oppositional Defiant Disorder (ODD)

SUGGESTIONS FOR USING THIS EXERCISE WITH STUDENT(S)

Students are constantly exposed to criticism, praise, and encouragement from their teachers, family members, and peers. These reactions to the student's behavior are often translated into an internal image of the self or the self-concept. Encouragement and specific, descriptive, or appreciative praise each contribute to healthy self-esteem, whereas criticism often demeans the student and deflates his or her self-image.

The activity asks the student to choose among several responses to criticism, praise, and encouragement. Both appropriate and inappropriate possibilities are listed. The intention is to involve the student in a discussion or thought process that considers socially appropriate responses that promote self-confidence and healthy self-esteem. This activity will help the student feel more comfortable when he or she is involved in an interaction that involves praise, criticism, or encouragement. The activity is appropriate for students in grades 4 through 12.

INSTRUCTIONS FOR THE STUDENT

Each day, you experience praise, criticism, and encouragement from your family, friends, and teachers. Encouragement happens when someone recognizes something about you or what you are doing and comments on it specifically. Your parent may notice when you pick up your clothes, help out a younger sibling, or work really hard on your homework. When they tell you how your efforts make a difference, that's encouragement. Praise tends to focus on a personal attribute, behavior, or talent. If your coach or teacher says you are really good at something, that is praise. Encouragement is nearly always appreciated and easy to handle, because it points exactly to what the person does that is appreciated. Praise is accepted and feels comfortable when it is sincere and when the person being praised agrees with it. Criticism focuses on a personal characteristic or behavior, but because it is negative, it almost always makes the person feel discouraged.

Learning how to respond to criticism, praise, and encouragement will help you feel confident when you receive praise and encouragement and help you to avoid feeling discouraged when you are criticized. The Responses to Criticism, Praise, and Encouragement activity offers you several possible options to use when someone comments on your personal attributes, behavior, or efforts. Circle the responses that will help you feel good about yourself while remaining polite and appropriate to the other person. There are five appropriate responses to criticism, two appropriate responses to praise, and four appropriate responses to encouragement.

After you circle the responses that will work for you, write some of your own responses in the spaces provided at the end of the activity. Discuss your ideas in your group session or individually with your counselor.

RESPONSES TO PRAISE, CRITICISM, AND ENCOURAGEMENT

Circle the appropriate responses.

Next Time I Am Criticized, I Will
1. Say, "It hurts my feelings when you criticize me. I wish you would stop."
2. Say, "It takes one to know one."
3. Say, "Would you be willing to help me improve?"
4. Walk away and find a more encouraging group or friend.
5. Try even harder to do a better job.
6. Give up because it's not worth the discouragement.
7. Say, "I'm sick of your constant criticism."
8. Walk away and pout.
9. Say, "Criticism makes this even harder."

Next Time I Am Praised, I Will
1. Say, "Thank you."
2. Say, "Oh, it was nothing."
3. Ask, "What specifically did you like?"
4. Say, "My friend did most of the work."

Next Time I Am Encouraged, I Will
1. Say, "Thanks for your help or support."
2. Say, "I really appreciate your comments."
3. Say, "I'm going to keep working on it."
4. Say, "Do you have any other suggestions?"

Now add some of your own ideas.

Responses to criticism:

_____

_____

_____

Responses to praise:

_____

_____

_____

Responses to encouragement:

_____

_____

_____

THE REWIND GAME

GOALS OF THE EXERCISE

1. Identify inappropriate personal behavior and responses that upset and frustrate others.
2. Rewrite inappropriate responses in positive terms.
3. Practice using appropriate behavior and responses with others.
4. Control impulsive, negative responses and replace them with positive actions.

ADDITIONAL PROBLEMS FOR WHICH THIS EXERCISE MAY BE MOST USEFUL

*   Anger Management/Aggression
*   Attention-Deficit/Hyperactivity Disorder (ADHD)
*   Conflict Management
*   Divorce
*   Social Maladjustment/Conduct Disorder

SUGGESTIONS FOR USING THIS EXERCISE WITH STUDENT(S)

Students who react or behave impulsively can benefit from looking at their actions and considering how they would behave if given another opportunity. The Rewind Game instructs the student to describe a scenario from personal experience, to identify an action that created a problem either for him- or herself or for another person, and to rewrite the personal response in more positive terms. This process will help the student understand that there are both appropriate and inappropriate methods of responding to any situation and that positive responses contribute to positive relationships and results, whereas negative responses create undesirable consequences.

The Rewind Game assigns 5 points for reworking a negative response in writing and 10 points for actually approaching the injured or upset person and asking for a chance to rewind and try a more positive method of dealing with the situation. Students can accumulate points as they rewind various scenarios and can designate their level of expertise based on the number of points they have earned. This activity is appropriate for students in grades 3 through 12 and can be adapted for use with younger students.

THE REWIND GAME

We often say or do things that we regret and wish that we had a chance to rewind and try again. The Rewind Game allows you to restate or redo an inappropriate comment or behavior and resolve a problem or issue with someone who was hurt or upset with your initial approach. In the space provided, describe several situations, including what you actually said or did, and a more appropriate rewind version for each. Show this activity sheet to the other involved person and ask if he or she would give you another chance.

Score 5 points for each situation you describe and rewind on this activity sheet. Score 10 points for each situation that you actually rewind with the other person. Scoring 0 to 10 points indicates that you are a rewind beginner; 10 to 30 points indicates that you are an intermediate-level rewind player; 30 or more points indicates that you are developing expert rewind skills.

Situation	What I Said or Did	My Rewind Version
Examples		
• *I wanted my mom to drive me home from school, and she said she would be a few minutes late.*	• *I blew up when she picked me up and called her selfish. I told her she didn't care about me and didn't love me. She said my words made her not want to pick me up at all.*	• *I will tell my mom that I get frustrated when she doesn't pick me up on time and that I am sorry for my hurtful words. I will thank her for taking the time to pick me up when I ask.*
• *I told my dad I would be home for dinner.*	• *I watched a video with a friend and completely lost track of the time. I was an hour late for dinner. My dad said I couldn't go out for the rest of the week.*	• *Next time, I will be sure to wear a watch or check a clock so I make it home on time for dinner.*

Situation	What I Said or Did	My Rewind Version
Situation		
Situation		
Situation		
Situation		

PROBLEM OWNERSHIP

GOALS OF THE EXERCISE

1. Identify personal problems that need to be solved.
2. Differentiate problems that the student can solve alone from those that require assistance.
3. Improve problem-solving abilities.
4. Identify others who can help solve personal problems.

ADDITIONAL PROBLEMS FOR WHICH THIS EXERCISE MAY BE MOST USEFUL

- Attachment/Bonding Deficits
- Attention-Deficit/Hyperactivity Disorder (ADHD)
- Conflict Management
- Divorce
- Responsible Behavior Training

SUGGESTIONS FOR USING THIS EXERCISE WITH STUDENT(S)

Students sometimes feel overwhelmed and incapable of solving their problems. It is helpful if they can differentiate between problems that can be solved by themselves and those that require assistance from family, friends, teachers, or mentors. The Problem Ownership activity asks the student to identify several problems that are of personal concern. The problems are to be listed as those that can be solved by the student alone and those that will require assistance from another person. The student is then instructed to draw a picture of a problem that he or she has already solved and to describe the problem in writing in the spaces following the picture. This will help the student recognize his or her problem-solving abilities and encourage and empower the student to think constructively about how to solve current problems.

The last part of the activity instructs the student to draw a picture of a problem that needs to be solved. Following the picture the student is asked to determine if this problem can be solved alone or if he or she will need help in solving it. If help is needed, the student is asked to identify people who could provide the help. When the activity is completed, discuss with the student how to ask for help from one of the people he or she has listed. The activity can be shared with the parents to enhance their awareness of the student's improving problem-solving skills and to encourage them to offer help when necessary. This activity is appropriate for students in grades kindergarten through 5.

PROBLEM OWNERSHIP

Some problems I can solve alone, but other problems I need help in solving. When I have a problem, I feel best if I can figure it out alone or with assistance from another responsible person. Solving problems helps me to feel capable and responsible. List some problems that you can solve alone and some that you need help to solve.

Problems I Can Solve Alone	**Problems I Need Help to Solve**
_____	_____
_____	_____
_____	_____
_____	_____

Draw a picture of a problem you have solved:

Describe the problem _____

_____

Draw a picture of a problem that needs to be solved:

This is a problem I can solve alone _____ or one I need help with _____

Describe the problem: _____

_____

_____

_____

Who can help me with this problem?

_____

_____

_____

_____

_____

_____

MY SECRET STORY

GOALS OF THE EXERCISE

1. Disclose the story of child abuse by using the process of journaling.
2. Identify thoughts and feelings connected with the abuse in a supportive, therapeutic environment.
3. Clarify how the abuse has affected all aspects of the student's life.
4. Identify support systems available to help the student deal with the ramifications of the abuse.
5. Prepare the student for dealing with the abuse and moving ahead with life.

ADDITIONAL PROBLEMS FOR WHICH THIS EXERCISE MAY BE MOST USEFUL

- Grief/Loss
- Divorce
- Depression
- Self-Esteem Building
- Suicide Ideation/Attempt

SUGGESTIONS FOR USING THIS EXERCISE WITH STUDENT(S)

Students who have experienced physical or sexual abuse may find it difficult to disclose their personal thoughts and feelings even to a supportive therapist. The My Secret Story activity encourages the student to record his or her personal ideas privately—in writing—and then share them with the therapist during a counseling session. *Journaling* allows the student to record his or her reactions before disclosing them. The activity lists 24 journal-entry starters to help the student describe the story of abuse sequentially and consider the most common and relevant aspects of abuse on minors. Space is provided for the student to note additional comments and concerns. Instruct the student to complete as many of the questions each week as he or she feels comfortable with. The student who finds it difficult to write in this activity may need initial assistance during the therapy session.

The activity is designed to encourage the process of journaling during the period of disclosure and its continuation thereafter. Journaling is highly recommended as an intervention to address traumatic experiences, as well as the more normal daily ups and downs of life. This activity is appropriate for students in grades 4 through 12 and can be adapted for use with younger students with additional assistance from the counselor.

MY SECRET STORY

Writing down your thoughts and feelings can help you sort out many difficult, challenging, scary, or traumatic experiences in your life. This is especially true of any type of child abuse. By writing down, in a story format or in a personal journal, the varied, sometimes extremely confusing feelings you experience as a result of the abuse, you will begin to understand and make sense of what happened, how the abuse has affected you, and how you will manage the difficult experience and go on from here. Your written words will help you to express yourself more clearly during your counseling or therapy sessions and during other times when you are asked to describe what happened and how you felt. Remember that your journal is private; only you can decide whether to share your personal notes. However, therapy will be much more effective if you are willing to share your written thoughts and feelings with your counselor.

This activity is just a beginning to help you establish the habit of journaling. If you journal regularly, you will find that you understand yourself better and are better prepared to deal with all of the events in your life. Complete the starter sentences in the following list to tell your personal story. If you have additional thoughts and responses to record, use the back of the pages or separate notepaper to describe all of the important aspects of your story.

Answer a few of the following questions each week to prepare for your counseling session. You may answer the questions in the order given or decide which ones to complete each week. Try to find a quiet, peaceful place to do your journaling. After you have completed all of the questions, continue the journaling process by responding to questions developed by yourself and your counselor or simply recording a couple of paragraphs that describe your personal experiences or feelings on each day.

1. Describe your life before the abuse occurred (e.g., your family, friends, school, activities, major interests). _____

   _____

   _____

   _____

   _____

   _____

2. Who did you love and trust the most before the abuse? (Why?) _____

_____

_____

_____

3. Who did you mistrust before the abuse? (Why?) _____

_____

_____

_____

_____

4. Who do you love and trust most now? (Why?) _____

_____

_____

_____

_____

5. What was your relationship with the perpetrator before the abuse? _____

_____

_____

_____

_____

6. When did the abuse first occur? _____

_____

_____

7. How long did the abuse go on? _____

_____

_____

8. Describe the abuse in your own words. _____

_____

_____

_____

_____

9. Describe your reactions during the abuse. _____

_____

_____

_____

_____

10. Describe your reactions after the abuse. _____

_____

_____

_____

_____

11. How was the abuse discovered? _____

_____

_____

_____

_____

12. How did you feel about disclosing the abuse? _____

_____

_____

_____

_____

13. Who helped you with the disclosure? (How did they help?) _____

_____

_____

_____

14. How did your family and friends react to the disclosure? _____

_____

_____

_____

15. Do you think someone could have prevented or stopped the abuse earlier? (Describe who and how.) _____

_____

_____

_____

16. How has your life changed as a result of the disclosure of the abuse? _____

_____

_____

_____

_____

17. What has happened to the perpetrator as a result of the abuse? _____

_____

_____

_____

_____

18. Do you think this is an appropriate consequence for the perpetrator? (Describe what you think would be appropriate.) _____

_____

_____

_____

_____

19. What would you like to say to the perpetrator now? _____

_____

_____

_____

_____

20. Who has helped you deal with the abuse? _____

_____

_____

_____

_____

21. Have you experienced feelings of guilt, regret, or remorse concerning the abuse? (Describe.) _____

_____

_____

_____

_____

MEASURING MY FEELINGS

GOALS OF THE EXERCISE

1. Identify negative feelings associated with experiencing child abuse.
2. Identify positive feelings experienced as recovery begins.
3. Measure the ebb and flow and the intensity of the feelings experienced.
4. Develop a sense of control over personal feelings and attitude.

ADDITIONAL PROBLEMS FOR WHICH THIS EXERCISE MAY BE MOST USEFUL

- Grief/Loss
- Conflict Management
- Divorce
- Depression
- Self-Esteem Building
- Suicide Ideation/Attempt

SUGGESTIONS FOR USING THIS EXERCISE WITH STUDENT(S)

Victims of child abuse often feel overwhelmed and lack a sense of control over their feelings and their lives. The Measuring My Feelings activity helps the student identify both the positive and the negative feelings experienced after the disclosure of the abuse and the intensity of these feelings as the weeks toward recovery progress. The student is asked to select personal feelings directly related to the abuse from a provided list and to graph the intensity of these feelings during the days between counseling sessions. The student follows the same process for positive feelings during the same time frame. The weekly graphs of feelings should be saved in a personal journal or notebook to track the ebb and flow of the feelings as the student learns to cope with the aftermath of the abuse.

The exercise is designed to help the student recognize that through counseling and strategies to cope with personal trauma, feelings and attitude become a matter of personal choice. With the help of the counselor, the student is instructed to determine whether appropriate progress toward acceptance and adjustment is being accomplished. This assessment should be made during a counseling session, where recognition can be given for progress that has been made or support and guidance can be given for lack of progress. This activity is appropriate for students in grades 5 through 12 and can be modified for use with younger students.

MEASURING MY FEELINGS

The following is a list of feelings commonly experienced by victims of child abuse. Look over the list and add any additional words that represent feelings you are aware of or experience often. Notice that the list contains a mixture of positive and negative feelings. Students who have been abused continue to experience pleasant and positive feelings along with their unpleasant and negative feelings of distress and victimization. Highlight or circle the feelings you are dealing with as a direct result of the abuse.

Abandoned	Embarrassed	Left out	Smart
Angry	Enraged	Lonely	Smug
Anxious	Excited	Lovestruck	Surprised
Ashamed	Exhausted	Loving	Suspicious
Badgered	Foolish	Mad	Uneasy
Betrayed	Frightened	Mischievous	Upset
Bored	Frustrated	Neglected	Uptight
Calm	Guilty	Nervous	Victimized
Cautious	Happy	Overwhelmed	Welcome
Chippy	Helpless	Proud	Worried
Confident	Hopeful	Sad	_____
Confused	Hopeless	Scared	_____
Curious	Horrified	Serene	_____
Depressed	Hysterical	Serious	_____
Disappointed	Important	Shamed	_____
Disgusted	Jealous	Shocked	_____
Ecstatic	Lazy	Shy	_____

It is normal to feel upset and extremely concerned after disclosing an abusive situation. However, these negative reactions tend to ebb and flow as you begin to deal with the abuse with the help of your counselor and supportive family members and friends.

As your counseling and adjustment progress, you will experience an increase in positive feelings and a decreased intensity of negative feelings. Eventually, it will become your decision whether to dwell on the negative feelings resulting from your past experience or to focus on the positive aspects of your life and experience joy and happiness once again.

Underline or highlight, using different colors, the positive feelings you occasionally experience now and hope to enjoy more frequently in the future. Use the graphs to measure the intensity of your positive and negative feelings over a one-week period. Compare the intensity of your positive and negative feelings from week to week to determine if your attitude and outlook is becoming more negative, remaining the same, or becoming more positive. Discuss the results with your counselor and decide together if you are making appropriate progress in coping with the aftereffects of the abuse.

Negative Feelings I Have Experienced During the Week of _____

Record eight negative feelings you have experienced this week on the lines following the graph. Estimate the level of intensity for each feeling by shading in the spaces up to the appropriate level: 0 to 30 is in the mild range of intensity, 30 to 60 is in the moderate range, and 60 to 80 is in the high range. The highest range—80 to 100—indicates that you are overwhelmed by the feeling.

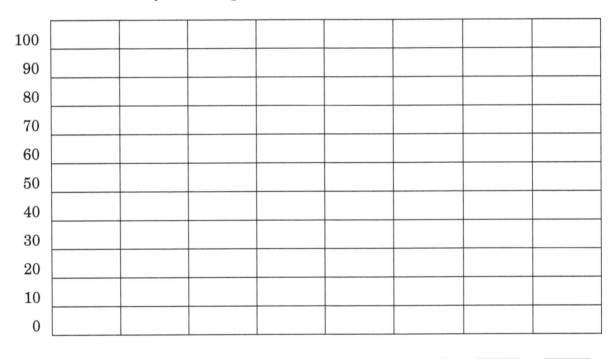

Positive Feelings I Have Experienced During the Week of _____

Record eight positive feelings you have experienced this week on the lines following the graph. Estimate the level of intensity for each feeling by shading in the spaces up to the appropriate level.

100								
90								
80								
70								
60								
50								
40								
30								
20								
10								
0								

_____   _____   _____   _____   _____   _____   _____   _____

BUILDING ON STRENGTHS

GOALS OF THE EXERCISE

1. Recognize that all people have strengths and weaknesses.
2. Identify personal attributes and talents.
3. Utilize strengths to achieve personal goals.
4. Identify developing strengths.

ADDITIONAL PROBLEMS FOR WHICH THIS EXERCISE MAY BE MOST USEFUL

- Academic Motivation
- Attachment/Bonding Deficits
- Depression
- Learning Difficulties
- Poverty/Economic Factors

SUGGESTIONS FOR USING THIS EXERCISE WITH STUDENT(S)

According to Gardner's theory of multiple intelligences, people are smart in different ways. All students have talents and abilities to a greater or lesser extent in various areas of functioning (e.g., artistic, musical, linguistic, mathematical, mechanical, personal, interpersonal, athletic), but they often fail to recognize their personal strengths. Awareness of personal strengths can help the student develop a positive self-concept and plan for future academic pursuits, leisure-time activities, and short- and long-term goal achievement.

The Building on Strengths activity instructs the student to identify personal abilities and to consult with significant others to gather more data if necessary. A discussion about personal attributes in the areas of multiple intelligences during a counseling session will prepare the student to apply this concept personally and begin the process of discovering his or her personal talents. These strengths are to be measured only on a personal level; they are not to be compared to the accomplishments of other students or family members. The activity is points out that no one has all of the listed attributes, but everyone has some. This activity is appropriate for students in grades 4 through 12.

BUILDING ON STRENGTHS

Each of us has strengths or personal talents that stand out as more skillful or more advanced than other abilities. For example, some people are musically talented but not so exceptional in athletics. Another person may be very friendly and social but have to work very hard to understand math. All people are a mixture of strong and weak abilities. When we set goals for ourselves, we need to consider our strengths and use them to help us achieve our goals.

The following is a list of positive characteristics. No one has all of these attributes, but everyone has some. Circle five or ten strengths that you already have or are working hard to develop. Check with your parents, teachers, counselor, or mentor to get additional information about your personal attributes. Write any additional personal strengths that aren't listed in the blank spaces provided.

Artistic	Enthusiastic	Math abilities
Athletic	Flexible	Mechanical
Attentive	Friendly	Musical
Attractive	Funny	Reading abilities
Computer skills	Good listener	Sensible
Considerate	Good memory	Sensitive
Cooperative	Good student	Spelling skills
Dependable	Good talker	Thoughtful
Determined	Intuitive	Try hard
Electronic abilities	Kind	Upbeat
Energetic	Loving	Writing abilities

_____   _____   _____

_____   _____   _____

_____   _____   _____

Now name a few of your short- and long-term goals. A short-term goal might be to improve spelling grades or to score well on the next math quiz; a long-term goal might be to graduate from high school or college or to pursue a specific career.

**Short-Term Goals
(Sometime This Year)**

_____

_____

_____

_____

**Long-Term Goals
(Sometime in the Next 10 Years)**

_____

_____

_____

_____

Choose one short-term and one long-term goal and identify the personal strengths you can use to achieve each goal. Write your short-term and your long-term goals and list the personal strengths that will be helpful to you in achieving these goals.

My Short-Term Goal

_____

**Personal Strengths I Will Use to
Achieve This Goal**

_____

_____

_____

_____

My Long-Term Goal

_____

**Personal Strengths I Will Use to
Achieve This Goal**

_____

_____

_____

_____

My Short-Term Goal

_____

**Personal Strengths I Will Use to
Achieve This Goal**

_____

_____

_____

_____

My Long-Term Goal

_____

**Personal Strengths I Will Use to
Achieve This Goal**

_____

_____

_____

_____

INSPIRATIONS

GOALS OF THE EXERCISE

1. Identify famous people who have disabilities.
2. Recognize that disabilities do not prevent recognition and accomplishment.
3. Draw inspiration from celebrities who have learned to manage their disabilities.
4. Identify mentors and role models in the family, school, and community.

ADDITIONAL PROBLEMS FOR WHICH THIS EXERCISE MAY BE MOST USEFUL

- Academic Motivation
- Divorce
- Depression
- Learning Difficulties
- Poverty/Economic Factors

SUGGESTIONS FOR USING THIS EXERCISE WITH STUDENT(S)

Students with disabilities and other personal challenges need role models and mentors to assist them in the transition from school to work and to provide inspiration and motivation for future success. Many famous people in sports, entertainment, academics, business, and politics have made major contributions to society despite physical, mental, or emotional challenges. The Inspirations activity lists 17 famous people with disabilities who have major accomplishments to their credit, such as climbing Mount Everest or winning an Olympic gold medal. The student is asked to match each celebrity's name with his or her accomplishment.

The student is then instructed to identify people in his or her family, school, or community who provide inspiration because of their attitude and accomplishments. These need not be famous people, but they should demonstrate the same courage and determination as the celebrities. Both groups provide role models for the student to admire and emulate. The list of local role models can provide additional inspiration and potential mentors to guide the student toward the fulfillment of his or her personal dreams and goals.

The completed worksheet can lead to further discussions, during individual or group counseling sessions, that focus on the accomplishments and achievements of people with personal challenges. This activity is appropriate for students in grades 3 through 12.

INSPIRATIONS

Many people with disabilities accomplish amazing feats and become inspirations to people with and without disabilities. These courageous people become role models and heroes by demonstrating dedication and determination despite the challenges they face. The following is a list of celebrities with various disabilities who have made major contributions to our society. They will be recognized and remembered for the goals they achieved and the disabilities they overcame. Place the letter of the accomplishment beside the celebrity's name. The answers are at the end of the exercise.

1.	Jim Abbott	_____	A.	Acclaimed violinist with paralyzed legs
2.	Chris Burke	_____	B.	Actor paralyzed from spinal injury
3.	Tom Cruise	_____	C.	Actor with Down syndrome
4.	Patty Duke	_____	D.	Actor with dyslexia
5.	Stephen Hawking	_____	E.	Actor with leg braces and crutches
6.	Henry Holden	_____	F.	Actress with manic-depressive disorder
7.	Magic Johnson	_____	G.	Athlete with HIV
8.	Marlee Matlin	_____	H.	Comedian and actress with hearing loss
9.	Terence Parkin	_____	I.	Football player paralyzed with spinal cord injury; advocate for research to cure paralysis.
10.	Itzhak Perlman	_____	J.	Legally blind Olympic track-and-field athlete
11.	Christopher Reeve	_____	K.	Major League Baseball pitcher without right hand
12.	Franklin Roosevelt	_____	L.	Miss America with profound hearing loss
13.	Wilma Rudolph	_____	M.	Track star and Olympic gold medal winner with deformed legs
14.	Marla Runyan	_____	N.	Olympic swimmer with hearing loss
15.	Mike Utley	_____	O.	Physics professor with ALS (amyotrophic lateral sclerosis, or Lou Gehrig's disease)
16.	Erik Weihenmayer	_____	P.	President with legs paralyzed from polio
17.	Heather Whitestone	_____	Q.	Climbed the summit of Mount Everest while legally blind

Now identify some role models and inspirational people you know personally in your family, school, or community. Write their names in column 1 and their disability and accomplishment(s) in column 2.

Name   **Accomplishment(s)**

_____   _____

_____   _____

_____   _____

_____   _____

Answers: 1. = K   2. = C   3. = D   4. = F   5. = O   6. = E   7. = G   8. = H   9. = N
10. = A   11. = B   12. = P   13. = M   14. = J   15. = I   16. = Q   17. = L

GOAL ACHIEVEMENT

GOALS OF THE EXERCISE

1. Recognize that planning is necessary for goal achievement.
2. Identify personal long- and short-term goals.
3. Recognize resources available to assist in goal attainment.
4. Develop and commit to a plan for goal achievement.

ADDITIONAL PROBLEMS FOR WHICH THIS EXERCISE MAY BE MOST USEFUL

*   Academic Motivation
*   Attachment/Bonding Deficits
*   Depression
*   Physical Disabilities
*   School Refusal/Phobia

SUGGESTIONS FOR USING THIS EXERCISE WITH STUDENT(S)

The Goal Achievement activity encourages the student to consider planning as an essential element in goal attainment rather than leaving the outcome to chance or to someone else's efforts. This activity empowers the student to become personally responsible for reaching his or her major and minor goals and aspirations. The steps for goal achievement are described on the student's instruction sheet, and a sample plan is provided to illustrate the process.

The activity will help the student name a specific goal and identify the resources available to help attain the goal and to determine potential roadblocks to success. The student is instructed to formulate the steps required to reach his or her goal, to commit to making a personal effort, and to sign and date the plan. The worksheet can be used repeatedly as the student prepares to work toward specific short- and long-term goals. The plans can be kept in a personal journal and reviewed with the counselor or a teacher to help the student recognize the elements of a successful plan and revise plans that are not successful. The process of planning and organizing for goal attainment is a skill that will benefit the student throughout his or her lifetime. This activity is appropriate for students in all grades, although students in early elementary school grades will need assistance from the counselor in writing or drawing and processing the steps toward goal achievement.

INSTRUCTIONS FOR THE STUDENT

All goals take planning, whether they're national goals, like putting an astronaut on the moon, or personal goals, like passing the next spelling quiz in school. There are important steps to achievement of both large and small personal goals. It is helpful to name your goal and then think about exactly how you will succeed. The steps involved in reaching your goal are as follows:

1. Name your goal.
2. List the resources and support available to help you reach your goal.
3. List any challenges or roadblocks that may interfere with reaching your goal.
4. Create a plan for reaching your goal by listing the steps necessary for success.
5. Write a statement that commits you to working toward your goal.

The following is an example of a goal achievement plan developed by a third grader.

My Goal: *To improve my math grade from a C to a B during the next six-week grading period.*

List some resources available to help you to achieve the goal:

My teacher said she would help me in class or during recess.

My uncle is good at math, and he could help me at home.

I could work on my math at home after supper.

I could study for my tests during the study time our teacher gives us in class.

I could correct all of the mistakes on my math papers and quizzes and ask my teacher to check my work.

List some roadblocks or challenges in achieving this goal:

Math is hard for me.

I would rather go out for recess than stay in and study with my teacher.

It's noisy at home after supper, and the TV makes it hard for me to concentrate.

My uncle isn't always home to help me.

Sometimes I don't concentrate very well during math class.

Create a strategy and list the steps involved in achieving your goal:

1. *I am going to try really hard to concentrate during math class.*

2. *I am going to ask my uncle which nights he can be home to help me with my math.*

3. *I will do my homework at the kitchen table where I can't see the TV and use earplugs if necessary to keep out the noise.*

4. *I will ask my teacher to help me during class so I don't have to stay in for recess.*

5. *I will correct all of the mistakes on my math papers and quizzes and ask my teacher to check my work.*

6. *I will keep track of all my math grades to make sure I am maintaining a B or better work*

7. *I will share my plan with my teacher and ask if he or she has any other suggestions.*

Write your commitment to achieving your goal: *I will give this plan my best shot and try really hard to maintain a B or better grade average in math. If I find that this plan isn't working, I will talk with my teacher or counselor and try to develop a better plan to help me succeed.*

Now write a plan for your own goal:

GOAL ACHIEVEMENT

My goal: _____

_____

List some resources available to help you to achieve the goal: _____

_____

_____

_____

List some roadblocks or challenges in achieving this goal: _____

_____

_____

_____

Create a strategy and list the steps involved in achieving this goal:

1. _____

2. _____

3. _____

4. _____

5. _____

6. _____

7. _____

8. _____

Write your commitment to achieving your goal: _____

_____

_____

_____

Signed: _____

Date: _____

HOME/SCHOOL RULES COMPARISON

GOALS OF THE EXERCISE

1. Recognize that various settings and circumstances have different standards for behavior.
2. Identify specific rules that apply at school and those that apply at home.
3. Demonstrate the ability to adjust to different standards for behavior in various settings.
4. Cooperate with school and classroom rules and discipline structure.

ADDITIONAL PROBLEMS FOR WHICH THIS EXERCISE MAY BE MOST USEFUL

- Academic Motivation
- Divorce
- Parenting Skills/Discipline
- Diversity/Tolerance Training
- Responsible Behavior Training
- School Refusal/Phobia

SUGGESTIONS FOR USING THIS EXERCISE WITH STUDENT(S)

Students come to school from various backgrounds, and their families may have rules and systems of discipline that are quite different from those of the school. The Home/School Rules Comparison activity helps the student define the similarities and differences between limits that are set at home and those that are set at school. Recognition that there are various standards for behavior established for specific settings and circumstances will help the student adjust to the separate requirements of school and home.

The student is instructed to state the rules or behavioral standards established at school and at home for 16 situations commonly experienced by school-aged children. The school rules can be brainstormed with a counseling group or as part of a classroom discussion; however, the home rules should be completed by the student working alone or consulting with his or her parents or counselor. After the rules have been completed, they should be reviewed in a counseling session or during a classroom presentation that focuses on the importance of following different rules in different circumstances.

School rules are designed to promote safe, smooth functioning of the school environment and to prepare students for success in their future careers. Home rules are established to promote family harmony and appropriate behavior in the neighborhood. The ability to adjust to different standards of behavior in various settings indicates the development of social awareness, flexibility, interpersonal skills, and self-control. This exercise is appropriate for students in grades 1 through 12.

HOME/SCHOOL RULES COMPARISON

The rules at home and the rules at school are often different. For example, at home you can probably watch TV and eat at the same time; however, at school eating must be done in the lunchroom or, on special occasions, in the classroom. Perhaps there are different rules for the way you talk to your teacher and to your parents, for where your belongings go, for when you can work and play, and so forth. Most people live with and follow two or more sets of rules. There are different rules for home, school, church, movie theaters, sports events, and restaurants. Understanding and learning to follow different rules for different situations helps you to be appropriate and successful in all of your experiences and activities. The following are some situations where the rules at home may differ from the rules at school. Write the school rule first; then write the home rule.

Rules at School   **Rules at Home**

Speaking to an Adult

_____   _____

_____   _____

Fighting

_____   _____

_____   _____

Where Food Is Eaten

_____   _____

_____   _____

Doing Chores or Schoolwork

_____   _____

_____   _____

Speaking to Your Siblings or Classmates

_____   _____

_____   _____

Rules at School   **Rules at Home**

Attitude and Behavior When Being Disciplined

_____   _____

_____   _____

Disses and Put-Downs

_____   _____

_____   _____

Taking Care of Belongings

_____   _____

_____   _____

Borrowing From Others

_____   _____

_____   _____

Interrupting

_____   _____

_____   _____

Sharing

_____   _____

_____   _____

Consequences for Inappropriate Behavior

_____   _____

_____   _____

Acceptable Use of Language

_____   _____

_____   _____

Table Manners

_____   _____

_____   _____

Rules at School   **Rules at Home**

Playground or Outdoor Behavior

_____   _____

_____   _____

Time for Work and Play

_____   _____

_____   _____

Who Makes and Enforces the Rules

_____   _____

_____   _____

TASK BUSTER

GOALS OF THE EXERCISE

1. Break down tasks into manageable steps.
2. Recognize the step-by-step process of task completion.
3. Acknowledge own ability to complete chores and assignments.
4. Improve attitude toward task completion.

ADDITIONAL PROBLEMS FOR WHICH THIS EXERCISE MAY BE MOST USEFUL

- Academic Motivation
- Attention-Deficit/Hyperactivity Disorder (ADHD)
- Career Planning
- Learning Difficulties
- Oppositional Defiant Disorder (ODD)
- Responsible Behavior Training

SUGGESTIONS FOR USING THIS EXERCISE WITH STUDENT(S)

Students often feel overwhelmed when confronted with tasks they view as complicated and unmanageable. The Task Buster activity helps the student to break down the chore or assignment into simpler steps so that the job can be mastered sequentially, which greatly improves the student's "can-do" attitude and ability to complete the task. The student is instructed to choose one school assignment and one chore from home to dissect into smaller steps. The steps are to be written in order under the task so that the student can follow them sequentially as he or she works toward completion. If the student has difficulty determining the sequential steps, the teacher, parent, or counselor can give assistance. When the task has been accomplished, the student is instructed to enter the date of completion and to ask the teacher or parent to sign the worksheet.

This activity can be used repeatedly by the student to help him or her accomplish many different tasks that he or she is responsible for completing. The activity will help the student finish current tasks more easily and prepare him or her for future career and adult life demands. This activity is appropriate for students in all grade levels.

TASK BUSTER

Name: _____   **Age:** _____

Most tasks, chores, and assignments are made up of several smaller steps that must be finished to complete the larger job. For example, making a bed involves straightening the sheets, pulling up the covers, putting the pillow on top, tucking in the covers, and putting on the bedspread. It is much easier to do a quality job when you understand what the smaller steps are. Choose one chore from home and one assignment from school that you are responsible for and write down the smaller steps that are necessary to complete each task. If you have been asked to complete a chore or assignment and you aren't sure of the smaller steps required, ask for help from your parent or teacher. Put a checkmark next to each smaller step when you have finished it. When you have completed each larger task, record the date and have your teacher or parent sign the worksheet under the task.

An Assignment I Need to Complete　　　　**Steps Involved for Task Completion**

_____

1. _____
2. _____
3. _____
4. _____
5. _____
6. _____
7. _____

Date completed: _____   **Teacher's signature:** _____

A Chore I Need to Complete   **Steps Involved for Task Completion**

_____

1. _____
2. _____
3. _____
4. _____
5. _____
6. _____
7. _____

Date completed: _____   Parent's signature: _____

PERSONAL ORGANIZATION CHART

GOALS OF THE EXERCISE

1. Inventory personal belongings.
2. Organize personal belongings.
3. Get rid of unwanted or unneeded possessions.
4. Determine appropriate storage space for personal possessions.

ADDITIONAL PROBLEMS FOR WHICH THIS EXERCISE MAY BE MOST USEFUL

- Anxiety Reduction
- Attachment/Bonding Deficits
- Career Planning
- Divorce
- School Refusal/Phobia

SUGGESTIONS FOR USING THIS EXERCISE WITH STUDENT(S)

As students become older, they acquire personal belongings that far exceed their capacity to organize and conveniently store these items. The Personal Organization Chart helps the student inventory his or her possessions and determine which things need to be organized and stored and which need to be thrown away. The organization of personal belongings is presented as a lifelong task that becomes more difficult as possessions accumulate. An organized storage plan helps the student take care of his or her belongings and locate items when they are needed. Learning to take care of personal belongings is a skill that will enable the student to meet personal, family, and career demands more responsibly and efficiently.

The student is instructed to list all personal belongings into categories such as toys, clothes, and school items. Then the student is asked to cross off from the list and throw away all items that are no longer needed and store his or her remaining possessions in an organized manner either at home or at school. Suggestions for storage areas are provided, and the student is asked to select from the list or indicate additional storage possibilities. The student is advised to check with his or her parent and/or teacher for approval of his or her personal storage plan. This activity is appropriate for students in all grade levels.

PERSONAL ORGANIZATION CHART

Organizing personal belongings is a lifelong responsibility. The older you become, the more stuff you will have to keep track of. Finding a place to keep your possessions is sometimes very challenging. It is helpful to make a list of everything you have and then determine which things you want to keep and which you can throw away. First, list your belongings in categories; cross off the things you no longer need and throw them away. Then, determine an appropriate place to keep the possessions you still want and need.

Toys and Games

_____ _____ _____

_____ _____ _____

_____ _____ _____

_____ _____ _____

_____ _____ _____

School Supplies

_____ _____ _____

_____ _____ _____

_____ _____ _____

Clothes

_____ _____ _____

_____ _____ _____

_____ _____ _____

_____ _____ _____

_____ _____ _____

Sports and Play Equipment

_____   _____   _____

_____   _____   _____

_____   _____   _____

_____   _____   _____

_____   _____   _____

_____   _____   _____

Personal Hygiene

_____   _____   _____

_____   _____   _____

_____   _____   _____

Music

_____   _____   _____

_____   _____   _____

_____   _____   _____

Transportation

_____   _____   _____

_____   _____   _____

Hobbies

_____   _____   _____

_____   _____   _____

_____   _____   _____

_____   _____   _____

Electronics (e.g., computers, CD players, radio, boom box)

_____   _____   _____

_____   _____   _____

_____   _____   _____

Books and Reading Materials

_____   _____   _____

_____   _____   _____

_____   _____   _____

Pictures and Memorabilia

_____   _____   _____

_____   _____   _____

_____   _____   _____

Other: _____

_____   _____   _____

_____   _____   _____

_____   _____   _____

Other: _____

_____   _____   _____

_____   _____   _____

_____   _____   _____

Other: _____

_____   _____   _____

_____   _____   _____

_____   _____   _____

Now that you have decided what to keep and have thrown away all of the stuff you no longer want or need, find a place to put your remaining belongings. The following are suggested storage places:

An old suitcase	Hooks in closet	Other: _____
An old trunk	Hooks in garage	_____
Boxes labeled according to content	Hooks in room	_____
	Laundry bag	_____
Cabinets in your room, basement, or garage	Locker at school	_____
Closet shelves or floor	On hangers	_____
Desk at home	Plastic bags hung on hooks	_____
Desk at school	Shelves or boxes in your basement	_____
Dresser drawers		_____
Flat boxes under your bed	Shelves in the garage	_____
Garage floor	Shelves in your room	
Hooks in basement	Your backpack	_____

List the categories of your belongings and determine where and how you will organize and store them. Be sure to check with your teacher and/or parents for their approval of your organized storage plan.

Category of Belonging	**Storage Place for Possessions**
_____	_____
_____	_____
_____	_____
_____	_____
_____	_____
_____	_____
_____	_____
_____	_____
_____	_____
_____	_____
_____	_____
_____	_____

ATTENDING SCHOOL SELF-REPORT

GOALS OF THE EXERCISE

1. Reduce resistance to attending school.
2. Reduce the amount of time spent in the before-school routine.
3. Track time spent in school by days and hours of the school day.
4. Increase school attendance.

ADDITIONAL PROBLEMS FOR WHICH THIS EXERCISE MAY BE MOST USEFUL

- Attention-Deficit/Hyperactivity Disorder (ADHD)
- Attention-Seeking Behavior
- Parenting Skills/Discipline
- Responsible Behavior Training

SUGGESTIONS FOR USING THIS EXERCISE WITH STUDENT(S)

Self-monitoring is a method of focusing the student's attention on personal actions that frequently results in a positive change in the behavior being monitored. The Attending School Self-Report outlines for the student the before-school routine and the school day and instructs the student to record the number of minutes spent getting ready for school and the number of minutes spent in school. The goal of the activity is to reduce the time spent getting to school and to increase the time spent in class and participating in school-related activities. This improvement will take place over time as the student begins to feel more in control as a result of the self-monitoring process. The chart and graph allows the student to intrinsically reward him- or herself as progress is recorded daily and weekly.

The charts should be signed by the student, teacher, and parent to further reinforce the student's improvement and to offer guidance in areas that remain problematic. The information on the weekly charts should be processed during counseling sessions to further develop the student's insight pertaining to school attendance. The charts should be kept from week to week in a school attendance journal to track progress and to indicate whether particular times of the year reveal unusual attendance patterns. This activity is appropriate for students in all grade levels.

ATTENDING SCHOOL SELF-REPORT
(STUDENT SELF-MONITORING ATTENDANCE RECORD)

Name: _____ **Grade:** _____

Teacher(s): _____

Dates of report: from _____ **to** _____

Use this self-report chart and graph to measure the time you spend getting ready for school and the time you spend in class or related activities for one week. This activity breaks down each school day into specific time slots so that you can monitor your highest and lowest periods of attendance. Use a watch or timer to check yourself for the amount of time it takes you to prepare for your school day. Write the time taken to get to school under the Morning Goodbye section; then record the minutes spent in class and other school-related activities in the Class Time section.

At the end of each day, add up your total time in school for that day and color or shade in the graph up to the level of the total minutes you spent in class and participating in before-school, after-school, and lunchtime activities. On Friday, total up the in-school hours for the entire week and record that number in the space provided on the chart and on the graph. Answer the questions about factors that influence your school participation, and sign the record once it is complete. Save your weekly self-monitoring charts to track your progress throughout the school year.

ACTIVITY OR TASK   TIME ON TASK

Morning Goodbye

Record the number of minutes you spent getting ready for school.

	Mon.	Tues.	Wed.	Thurs.	Fri.
Time spent getting ready:	_____	_____	_____	_____	_____
Time spent on breakfast:	_____	_____	_____	_____	_____
Time spent getting in car, bus, or walking to school:	_____	_____	_____	_____	_____
Time spent saying goodbye and getting to class:	_____	_____	_____	_____	_____
Time I arrived in class:	_____	_____	_____	_____	_____

ACTIVITY OR TASK   TIME ON TASK

Class Time

Record the number of minutes you participated in school or a related activity.

	Mon.	Tues.	Wed.	Thurs.	Fri.
Before-school activities	_____	_____	_____	_____	_____
Morning: First hour	_____	_____	_____	_____	_____
Morning: Second hour	_____	_____	_____	_____	_____
Morning: Third hour	_____	_____	_____	_____	_____
Lunchtime	_____	_____	_____	_____	_____
Afternoon: First hour	_____	_____	_____	_____	_____
Afternoon: Second hour	_____	_____	_____	_____	_____
Afternoon: Third hour	_____	_____	_____	_____	_____
After-school activities	_____	_____	_____	_____	_____

Add up the total time spent in school each day. Use a calculator or get assistance from your teacher if necessary.

Total Time Spent in School

	Mon.	Tues.	Wed.	Thurs.	Fri.
Number of hours:	_____	_____	_____	_____	_____
Number of half days:	_____	_____	_____	_____	_____
Number of whole days:	_____	_____	_____	_____	_____

Which day did you spend the *most* time in school? _____
Which day did you spend the *least* time in school? _____
The activity I liked best in this week was _____.
The activity I had the most difficulty with this week was _____.
Additional comments: _____

_____

_____

Now add up your total time on task for this week.
Hours: _____   Half days: _____   Whole days: _____

TIME IN SCHOOL GRAPH

Record the time you spent in school each day and for the total week on the following graph by coloring or shading in the rectangles. Use minutes for each day's participation and hours for the weekly total. Give yourself a star if you spend more than 300 minutes per day in school.

Time on Task (min.)	Mon.	Tues.	Wed.	Thurs.	Fri.	Weekly Hours Total	
300							36
270							32
240							28
210							24
180							20
150							16
120							12
90							8
60							4
30							

Student's signature: _____   Date: _____

Teacher's signature: _____

Teacher's comments: _____

_____

_____

Parent's signature: _____   Date: _____

Parent's comments: _____

_____

_____

DO I HAVE WHAT I NEED?

GOALS OF THE EXERCISE

1. Prepare for the school day.
2. List materials necessary for daily school success.
3. Record forgotten items on the materials checklist.
4. Develop planning and organizational skills.

ADDITIONAL PROBLEMS THIS EXERCISE MAY BE MOST USEFUL FOR

- Anxiety Reduction
- Attention-Seeking Behavior
- Parenting Skills/Discipline
- Responsible Behavior Training

SUGGESTIONS FOR USING THIS EXERCISE WITH STUDENT(S)

Feeling unprepared for school can contribute to a student's anxiety and phobic feelings about going to school. The Do I Have What I Need? activity helps the student prepare for the school day by organizing all of the materials that will be needed. The activity lists many materials commonly required by students for class participation and instructs the student to add additional items necessary for a successful school day in his or her particular school. The school day is broken down into nine segments, beginning with Before-School Activities and ending with Preparing to Go Home. The student is asked to list all materials required for completing assignments and participating in activities during each time frame.

The student is advised to complete the material's checklist and pack all of the necessary items for the school day the evening before. In the morning, the student should re-check that everything has been included. If the student gets to school without an important item, he or she should write that item on the list so that he or she will remember it the following day. This process puts the student in charge of preparing for school and helps him or her develop self-reliance, organizational skills, and a feeling of empowerment that will enable him or her to overcome feelings of insecurity about school attendance. This activity is appropriate for students in all grade levels.

DO I HAVE WHAT I NEED?

Part of feeling confident about attending school is making sure you have what you need to be successful in school that day. The process of getting organized makes participating in any activity much easier. It is helpful to think about the school day in small segments and to list what you may need for each class or hour of the day. Start by listing the activities you have and the materials you will need for each. Some essentials for school success are listed as follows, but you will need to add to the list to make it fit your unique situation in your particular school.

Assignments	Crayons	Musical instrument
Backpack	Eraser	Notebooks
Bike	Games or toys	Paper
Bike lock	Gloves	Pencils
Books	Gym clothes	Permission slips
Boots	Gym shoes	Planner
Class project	Homework	Snack
Coat	Lunch	Sports equipment
Computer disks	Lunch money	Sweater

Add some materials you will need for a successful school day:

_____   _____   _____

_____   _____   _____

_____   _____   _____

_____   _____   _____

Now determine what you will need for each school day during the following week:

Before-School Activities
Example: Riding the bus

Materials I Will Need
Example: Games or toys

_____   _____

_____   _____

_____   _____

First-Hour Activities

Example: Teacher takes lunch count

_____

_____

_____

Materials I Will Need

Example: Lunch money or packed lunch

_____

_____

_____

Second-Hour Activities

Example: Language arts

_____

_____

_____

Materials I Will Need

Example: Homework, paper, pencils

_____

_____

_____

Third-Hour Activities

Example: Physical education

_____

_____

_____

Materials I Will Need

Example: Gym clothes and shoes

_____

_____

_____

Lunch-Hour Activities

Example: Eat lunch

_____

_____

_____

Materials I Will Need

Example: Lunch ticket or packed lunch

_____

_____

_____

After-Lunch First-Hour Activities

Example: Computer class

_____

_____

_____

Materials I Will Need

Example: Computer disk and book

_____

_____

_____

After-Lunch Second-Hour Activities

Example: Music class

_____

_____

_____

Materials I Will Need

Example: Musical instrument

_____

_____

_____

After-Lunch Third-Hour Activities

Example: Math class

_____

_____

_____

Materials I Will Need

Example: Homework, book, pencils, paper

_____

_____

_____

Preparing to Go Home

Example: Bus ride home

_____

_____

_____

Materials I Will Need

Example: Assignments, books, backpack, coat

_____

_____

_____

Create your personal list and organize your materials for school the night before when you go to bed. In the morning, check yourself to make sure you have what you need to be successful that day. This process will help you feel prepared and confident about going to school. Take the list with you to school. If you forgot something, add that item to the list so that you remember it the next day. Gradually, you will find that you are becoming more organized, and being more organized will add to your enjoyment of school and related activities.

SCHOOL DAYS IN A PERFECT WORLD

GOALS OF THE EXERCISE

1. Design the ideal school day.
2. Visualize self as successfully participating in school.
3. Compare an actual school day with an idealized school day.
4. Identify strategies for improving the school experience.

ADDITIONAL PROBLEMS FOR WHICH THIS EXERCISE MAY BE MOST USEFUL

- Anxiety Reduction
- Career Planning
- Learning Difficulties
- Poverty/Economic Factors

SUGGESTIONS FOR USING THIS EXERCISE WITH STUDENT(S)

Designing the perfect school day can help the student picture him- or herself as successfully participating in the school curriculum. The School Days in a Perfect World activity instructs the student to imagine a perfect school day and then to write a story involving the idealized experience. Sentence starters are provided to help the student organize and construct the story if necessary. The student is asked to write another short story describing a typical school day. Again, the student is free to use original ideas or incorporate the sentence starters into his or her story.

Finally, the student is instructed to compare the two stories and determine how aspects of the ideal school day could be incorporated into an actual school day. Six follow-up questions focus on the similarities and differences between the two days and strategies that the student can implement to produce an improved reality for him- or herself at school. This activity can create a sense of control over the positive and negative aspects of school and help empower the student to make changes in the perceived negative factors of his or her school experience. The stories and responses to the follow-up questions should be processed at a subsequent counseling session. This activity is appropriate for students in grades 3 through 12; with younger children, it can be used as a verbal storytelling exercise.

SCHOOL DAYS IN A PERFECT WORLD

Take a little time to dream about the perfect school day. What would this day look, sound, smell, and feel like? Describe this school day from the moment you wake up until the time you arrive back home from school: Who is the first person you see after you wake up? What do you have for breakfast? What do you wear? How do you get to school? What does your teacher say to you? Use some of the following sentence starters to write a story about the perfect school day, or if you prefer, you may write the story on your own. Try to include as many ideas as possible about things you would like to happen; this will help you positively influence your actual school days. After you have written about the perfect school day, write a story describing a typical school day, either on your own or using the sentence starters.

I wake up at . . . (time) when . . . (what wakes you up)	At lunch . . .
The first person I see is . . . who says . . .	I eat my favorite lunch, which is . . .
For breakfast I have . . .	After lunch . . .
My breakfast is fixed for me by . . .	During recess . . .
I get dressed and put on . . .	After recess . . .
I get to school using my favorite transportation, which is . . .	Other things we do in the afternoon are . . .
When I get to school, the first thing I do is . . .	I get to work with . . .
The first person in school I see is . . . who says . . .	My favorite activity today was . . .
When I get to my classroom, my teacher says . . .	On the way home . . .
We begin my favorite activity, which is . . .	After my perfect day I want to . . .
The next thing I do is . . .	I hope that tomorrow . . .
Other things we do in the morning are . . .	

My Perfect Day in School

_____
_____
_____
_____
_____
_____
_____
_____

A Typical Day in School

_____
_____
_____
_____
_____
_____
_____
_____

Now compare your perfect school day with a typical school day.

The major difference between a perfect school day and a typical school day is

_____
_____

The first thing about my typical school day I would like to change is

_____
_____

Some things in my perfect school day that happen in a typical school day are

_____
_____

Some things about my typical school day that I would like to continue are

_____
_____

Something I could do to make my dream school day more real is to

_____

_____

Another thing I could do to make my ideal school day more real is to

_____

_____

IDENTIFY AND SCHEDULE PLEASANT ACTIVITIES

GOALS OF THE EXERCISE

1. Identify, schedule, and participate in enjoyable activities.
2. Utilize behavioral strategies to overcome depression.
3. Enjoy the pleasant feelings that social, leisure, and recreational activities can bring.
4. Report a lift in mood resulting from increased social and recreational activity.
5. Alleviate depressed mood and return to previous level of effective functioning.

ADDITIONAL PROBLEMS FOR WHICH THIS EXERCISE MAY BE MOST USEFUL

- Depression
- Grief/Loss
- Divorce
- Suicide Ideation/Attempt

SUGGESTIONS FOR PROCESSING THIS EXERCISE WITH THE CLIENT

The student's depression may interfere with his or her ability to recall pleasant activities, and he or she may censor many of these activities, feeling that he or she does not have the energy for them. Encourage him or her to brainstorm freely. If it is necessary, this assignment can be done within the counseling session rather than relying on the reduced motivation of the depressed student to fulfill the requirements of the assignment. Perhaps the brainstorming and scheduling need to be done within the session and the homework is that of implementing the activity and recording its impact. It is recommended that the student monitor his or her mood before, during, and after the event to focus him or her on the positive effect that the event has on his or her mood. Review and reinforce the student's success in improving his or her mood using the satisfying activities.

* This exercise originates from Jongsma, A. E., Peterson, L. M., & McInnis, W. P. (in press). *Adult Psychotherapy Homework Planner* (5th ed.). Hoboken, NJ: Wiley. Reprinted with permission.

IDENTIFY AND SCHEDULE PLEASANT ACTIVITIES

Students who are depressed almost always withdraw from participation in activities that they once found satisfying, rewarding, pleasurable, or just plain fun. It is very important to break this cycle of withdrawal and to begin reinvesting in the activities of life, the relationships around you, and the things you do well. A starting point for this task of reinvestment or reinvolvement is to create an inventory of all those things that you found to be pleasant events in the past.

1. On the lines that follow, write down a description in only a few words of those activities that you found pleasurable and pleasant in the past. These enjoyable activities should include (1) positive social interactions (e.g., spending time with a good friend), (2) useful or productive activities (e.g., caring for your child, doing a job well), and (3) intrinsically pleasant activities (e.g., a meal at your favorite restaurant, listening to favorite music, taking a warm bath). During this brainstorming session, allow yourself to freely recall any pleasant and enjoyable activities without censoring them based on whether you think you have the energy for them or whether they are feasible. You may want to ask significant others to give input to your list, but please remember that this is your list of personal pleasant activities and must reflect events that you find enjoyable.

Positive Social Interactions	Useful Activities	Intrinsically Pleasant Activities
_____	_____	_____
_____	_____	_____
_____	_____	_____
_____	_____	_____
_____	_____	_____
_____	_____	_____
_____	_____	_____
_____	_____	_____
_____	_____	_____
_____	_____	_____

2. Now select from your list of pleasant events seven that you believe you are most likely to engage in. In the seven lines, list those activities, and then to the right of the activity, write a few words that describe what was positive about the activity or why you found it pleasant or enjoyable.

Most Likely Activities   **Why Pleasant?**

1. _____   _____
2. _____   _____
3. _____   _____
4. _____   _____
5. _____   _____
6. _____   _____
7. _____   _____

3. On the following lines, schedule one pleasant activity per day to which you are committed. Include the time of the day and with whom you might share the activity.

Activity   **When and With Whom**

Day 1 _____   _____
Day 2 _____   _____
Day 3 _____   _____
Day 4 _____   _____
Day 5 _____   _____
Day 6 _____   _____
Day 7 _____   _____

4. On the following lines, record the activity engaged in and the degree of satisfaction on a scale of 1 (low) to 10 (high) that was felt during and after the engagement with the pleasant event. Also record the effect that the pleasant event had on your mood using a scale of 1 (no positive effect) to 10 (strong uplifting effect on mood).

Activity   **Satisfaction**   **Effect on Mood**

Day 1 _____   _____   _____
Day 2 _____   _____   _____
Day 3 _____   _____   _____
Day 4 _____   _____   _____
Day 5 _____   _____   _____
Day 6 _____   _____   _____
Day 7 _____   _____   _____

REFRAMING YOUR WORRIES

GOALS OF THE EXERCISE

1. Verbalize an understanding of the reframing process.
2. Reframe situations that have triggered feelings of fear, anger, or anxiety.
3. Create encouraging and supportive self-talk to address stressful situations.
4. Identify the positive aspects of a challenging problem or situation.

ADDITIONAL PROBLEMS FOR WHICH THIS EXERCISE MAY BE MOST USEFUL

- Anger Management/Aggression
- Conflict Management
- Depression
- Divorce
- Grief/Loss

SUGGESTIONS FOR USING THIS EXERCISE WITH STUDENT(S)

This activity is based on the rational emotive techniques outlined in *A New Guide to Rational Living* by Ellis and Harper. The activity can be used to help students deal with a variety of problems and is applicable to most of the therapeutic areas addressed in *The School Counseling and School Social Work Treatment Planner* by Knapp and Jongsma. Students who experience high anxiety and low self-esteem and who lack problem-solving skills tend to catastrophize their problems, interpersonal relationships, and lives in general. Their self-talk becomes very negative and discouraging, and soon they see themselves as incapable of dealing with any challenging situation. Feelings of helplessness and hopelessness overwhelm these students and interfere with any attempt to seek help or effectively work out the problem alone.

The reframing process (e.g., reassessing a difficult situation from a different perspective that focuses on a more positive or solution-oriented approach) can help students gain a sense of self-control and personal power. Begin by brainstorming with the student a list of problems that he or she faces. Ask him or her to record these problems in the Situation column of the activity sheet. Next, have the student describe and record the worst-case scenario for each problem. Finally, ask the student to determine and record a positive yet realistic approach to the problem. This activity is appropriate for students in grades 7 through 12 and can be adapted for use with younger students.

INSTRUCTIONS FOR THE STUDENT

Use the reframing chart that follows to record one or more of your worries from a catastrophizing and a realistic/positive perspective. This will help you recognize that your point of view greatly influences whether you view a problem as manageable or beyond your control.

After you have analyzed one or more initial problems, begin to apply this approach to several additional situations throughout the week and use the activity sheet to record the process of moving from a helpless to an empowered state of mind. Discuss each recorded scenario with your counselor during subsequent counseling sessions. The following is an example of using this approach to problem solving:

Situation	Catastrophizing	Realistic/Positive
I lost my boyfriend.	*There is nothing I can do. I cry all the time. I can't focus on my studies. I'll never find another true love. I have to get him back. He thinks I'm a loser. All my friends will drop me. He's my whole life. I have no reason to live.*	*I'm lonely, but I'm also young and fun. I have other friends. It'll be hard, but I can get through this. There are plenty of other boys. I wasn't ready to get serious anyway. Perhaps he wasn't the right one for me.*

REFRAMING YOUR WORRIES

Record several of your prominent worries, a worst-case scenario, and an optimistic solution-oriented approach for each. Try to think of as many positive ways to consider the problem as possible.

Situation	Catastrophizing	Realistic/Positive

MY PERSONAL PROFILE

GOALS OF THE EXERCISE

1. Complete first-session icebreaker.
2. Establish student/counselor rapport.
3. Obtain basic personal information.
4. Develop student self-awareness.
5. Group interaction and bonding.

ADDITIONAL PROBLEMS FOR WHICH THIS EXERCISE MAY BE MOST USEFUL

- Academic Motivation
- Anxiety Reduction
- Conflict Management
- Learning Difficulties
- Physical Disabilities/Challenges

SUGGESTIONS FOR USING THIS EXERCISE WITH STUDENT(S)

The first session with a student or a group of students can set the tone for a positive, trusting relationship and create a willingness to disclose and discuss problems and work toward a solution. Trust is built while discussing subjects of interest to the student. This process also lays the groundwork for exploration of deeper, more sensitive issues to be addressed in future sessions. When used with group counseling sessions, this exercise can help group members develop awareness and empathy toward one another's situations. Ask the students to choose information to share from their worksheet. When working individually with a student, ask him or her to fill in one section at a time; then process the information from that section with him or her. With younger students, assistance can be given with the writing. This exercise can become the first entry of a personal journal kept by the student(s) during the counseling sessions. This exercise is appropriate for students in all grade levels.

MY PERSONAL PROFILE

Name _____

Address

_____

_____

_____

_____

Phone _____

Description

_____

_____

_____

_____

Family (Names, Ages, Relationship)

_____

_____

_____

_____

School (Grade, Teacher, Favorite Subject)

_____

_____

_____

_____

Additional Comments About School

_____

_____

_____

_____

_____

_____

My Favorite Color _____

My Special Hobbies

_____

_____

_____

_____

_____

Additional Comments About Your Family

_____

_____

_____

_____

Books I Enjoy

_____

_____

_____

_____

Pets

_____

_____

_____

_____

Friends

_____

_____

_____

My Favorite Foods

_____

_____

_____

_____

Vacations (Places I Have Gone or Places I Would Like to Go)

_____

_____

_____

_____

Some Things I Believe In

_____

_____

_____

_____

SKILL ASSESSMENT

GOALS OF THE EXERCISE

1. Identify currently mastered skills.
2. Recognize areas of personal abilities.
3. Accept the process of lifelong skill development.
4. Develop an awareness of skills required for future success.

ADDITIONAL PROBLEMS FOR WHICH THIS EXERCISE MAY BE MOST USEFUL

- Attention-Seeking Behavior
- Career Planning
- Learning Difficulties
- Responsible Behavior Training

SUGGESTIONS FOR USING THIS EXERCISE WITH STUDENT(S)

An awareness of talents and abilities in specified areas of functioning or multiple intelligences (see *Frames of Mind: The Theory of Multiple Intelligences* by Gardner) will allow the student to recognize personal strengths. Once identified, these strengths can be enhanced and extended to develop weaker areas of aptitude. An increased awareness of personal strengths will provide the student with a foundation for enhanced academic motivation and career planning while allowing him or her to build self-esteem and personal responsibility.

Ask the student to identify several personal skills in each ability area of multiple intelligences (e.g., mechanical, social, academic, musical, athletic). Have the student designate skills that he or she has mastered, skills that he or she is currently learning, and skills that he or she will need in the future. Encourage the student to list as many skills as possible, and offer assistance using the brainstorming process if necessary. The student is then asked to identify the skill area in which he or she has developed the most talent, the area that is most useful in school, the area that is most enjoyable, and the area that will be most important for future success. This exercise will help the student view skill building in various areas as an important, ongoing process which extends throughout one's lifetime.

After the skills have been listed, assign the student to draw a picture or paste a photo of a skill now mastered, a skill in progress, and a skill necessary for future success. This activity will reinforce the skill-building process and help the student develop a positive image of his or her skill-building attributes. This exercise is appropriate for students in grades 3 through 12.

SKILL ASSESSMENT

A skill is the ability to do something well. Skills make us feel capable and confident. Each of us has skills in several areas. List some of the capabilities or talents you have right now in the five skill areas listed below; then write some skills you are learning and some skills you will need in the future. When you have finished, identify the skill area in which you have the most talent, the skill area that you enjoy the most, the skill area that you use most in school, and the skill area that will be most important to you after you leave school and go to work. Then draw three pictures of yourself using or developing a skill that you have listed.

Mechanical (Building)	Social/ Emotional	Academic/ Learning	Musical/ Artistic	Athletic

Skills I Have Now

_____ _____ _____ _____ _____

_____ _____ _____ _____ _____

_____ _____ _____ _____ _____

_____ _____ _____ _____ _____

_____ _____ _____ _____ _____

Skills I Am Learning

_____ _____ _____ _____ _____

_____ _____ _____ _____ _____

_____ _____ _____ _____ _____

_____ _____ _____ _____ _____

_____ _____ _____ _____ _____

Skills I Will Need in the Future

_____ _____ _____ _____ _____

_____ _____ _____ _____ _____

_____ _____ _____ _____ _____

_____ _____ _____ _____ _____

_____ _____ _____ _____ _____

Identify the skill area in which you have the most talent, the skill area that you enjoy the most, the skill area that you use most in school, and the skill area that will be most important to you in the future.

_____   _____   _____   _____

PERSONAL SKILLS

Draw a picture or paste a photo of a skill you now have:

```
┌─────────────────────────────────────────────────────────┐
│                                                         │
│                                                         │
│                                                         │
│                                                         │
│                                                         │
│                                                         │
└─────────────────────────────────────────────────────────┘
```

Draw a picture or paste a photo of yourself learning a skill:

```
┌─────────────────────────────────────────────────────────┐
│                                                         │
│                                                         │
│                                                         │
│                                                         │
│                                                         │
│                                                         │
└─────────────────────────────────────────────────────────┘
```

Draw a picture or paste a photo of a skill you hope to develop in the future:

```
┌─────────────────────────────────────────────────────────┐
│                                                         │
│                                                         │
│                                                         │
│                                                         │
│                                                         │
│                                                         │
└─────────────────────────────────────────────────────────┘
```

MY PERSONAL SEXUAL RESPONSIBILITY CODE

GOALS OF THE EXERCISE

1. Commit to ethical sexual behavior.
2. Seek sexual information from knowledgeable, responsible sources.
3. Define *sexual integrity*.
4. Make positive choices concerning sexual behavior.

ADDITIONAL PROBLEMS FOR WHICH THIS EXERCISE MAY BE MOST USEFUL

- Responsible Behavior Training
- Self-Esteem Building
- Social Maladjustment/Conduct Disorder
- Social Skills/Peer Relationships
- Substance Abuse
- Teen Pregnancy

SUGGESTIONS FOR USING THIS EXERCISE WITH STUDENT(S)

The My Personal Sexual Responsibility Code activity explores with the student the meaning of sexual integrity and helps the student develop a personal standard for ethical sexual behavior. Students often neglect to define their personal values, especially in the area of sexual responsibility. This leads to impulsive and reactive sexual behavior that is frequently detrimental to the student's physical and emotional health and jeopardizes future plans and aspirations. Irresponsible sexual behavior can result in teen pregnancy, sexually transmitted diseases, abusive behavior toward others, low self-esteem, and lack of interest in school and other healthy, age-appropriate activities.

The activity defines the rationale for developing a sexual responsibility code and offers several examples of standards that adolescents typically choose as part of their commitment to healthy sexual behavior. Additional standards are to be developed by the student alone or through brainstorming in a school-sponsored sexuality class or counseling group. The student is instructed to write his or her own personal code, which is to be reviewed with the teacher or counselor to make any necessary revisions and then signed and dated by the student. The student is advised to keep the personal code in a private place where it can be read and considered frequently. The code can be discussed during counseling sessions and should be revised as needed. This activity is appropriate for students in grades 7 through 12.

MY PERSONAL SEXUAL RESPONSIBILITY CODE

To treat yourself and others with regard, respect, and responsibility, it is important to develop a code of ethics or values that can guide your decisions and behaviors. This is especially important in the area of sexual responsibility. Sexual integrity means acting with honesty, sincerity, and ethics when making choices that will affect yourself and others in the immediate future and for years to come. Consider some of the following statements, which are examples of values that other adolescents have incorporated into their personal sexual responsibility commitments. You may reword these statements and add additional values to define your own code of sexual behavior. Write your own personal sexual responsibility code to express your positive intentions in the area of ethical sexual behavior. When your code is complete, review it with your sex education teacher or your counselor and revise your statements as needed. Indicate your commitment to sexual integrity by signing the code. Keep your code with you in a private place and review it frequently to ensure that you use sexual responsibility when relating to others.

The following are statements that define responsible sexual behavior:

- I will abstain from sexual intercourse until I am ready to begin my family.
- I will protect myself and others from the possibility of contracting a sexually transmitted disease.
- I will protect myself and others from the possibility of getting pregnant.
- I will treat myself and others with respect when it comes to making sexual decisions.
- I will never try to force my sexual intentions on others.
- I will take sexual education seriously and attempt to learn as much about adolescent sexuality as possible from a credible source, such as school-, church-, or community-sponsored classes.
- I will address my questions about sexuality to knowledgeable and respected adults (e.g., parents, teachers, counselors, doctors, religious advisors).
- I will not rush my sexual maturation process and will relate to others in a friendly, age-appropriate manner that promotes healthy relationships with students of both sexes.
- I will seek medical advice whenever I have physical questions or concerns about my sexuality.

Add some responsible statements of your own for your personal responsibility code:

- _____
- _____
- _____
- _____
- _____
- _____

Now write your personal code. When you have completed it and reviewed it with a responsible adult (e.g., parent, counselor, sex education teacher, religious advisor), sign it and keep it where you can read and think about it often.

MY PERSONAL SEXUAL RESPONSIBILITY CODE

_____

_____

_____

_____

_____

_____

_____

_____

_____

_____

_____

_____

_____

_____

_____

_____

_____

_____

_____

_____

_____

_____

Signed: _____

Date: _____

CONTROL OF MY SEXUALITY
AND HEALTHY SELF-ESTEEM

GOALS OF THE EXERCISE

1. Gain a sense of control over positive and negative relationships.
2. Recognize the symptoms of healthy and unhealthy relationships.
3. Identify the connection between relationships and self-esteem.
4. Learn assertive responses to put-downs and harassment.

ADDITIONAL PROBLEMS FOR WHICH THIS EXERCISE MAY BE MOST USEFUL

- Responsible Behavior Training
- Self-Esteem Building
- Social Maladjustment/Conduct Disorder
- Social Skills
- Substance Abuse
- Teen Pregnancy

SUGGESTIONS FOR USING THIS EXERCISE WITH STUDENT(S)

The Control of My Sexuality and Healthy Self-Esteem activity defines for the student the attributes of healthy and unhealthy relationships and the effects of each on self-esteem. Unhealthy relationships are characterized as contributing to feelings of discouragement, disrespect, self-doubt, and low self-esteem, whereas positive relationships are characterized as supportive, caring, and encouraging to healthy self-esteem. First, the student is instructed to list several important personal relationships and describe the characteristics of each friendship. Then, the student is guided to categorize the relationships as having a positive or negative influence on his or her emotional health. Finally, the student is asked to determine how to deal with both the positive and the negative relationships in his or her life.

The activity offers techniques for dealing with the harassment and put-downs common to unhealthy relationships. The student is instructed to develop a strategy for responding to disrespectful comments and attempts to demean or humiliate. By learning assertive techniques for defusing harassment, the student will move out of the victim's role and into the more self-confident role of choosing relationships that support a healthy emotional state. The activity should be discussed with the student either individually or during a group session. This activity is appropriate for students in grades 7 through 12.

CONTROL OF MY SEXUALITY
AND HEALTHY SELF-ESTEEM

Students with a healthy self-esteem usually choose healthy relationships, whereas students with low self-esteem choose unhealthy relationships that further reduce their level of self-respect. One of the best ways to improve your level of self-esteem is to choose friendships and relationships that support your personal strengths, encourage your successes, and give you a sense of empowerment. If you are associated with friends who focus on your weaknesses and contribute to feelings of insecurity, helplessness, and hopelessness, possibly it is time to reevaluate why you allow these relationships to be part of your life. The following are two lists of words: the first describing healthy relationships and the second, unhealthy or abusive relationships.

1. Healthy relationships involve

Accountability	Ethics	Openness
Caring	Fairness	Shared responsibility
Communication	Honesty	Support
Compromise	Independence	Trust
Equality	Individuality	Win/win results
Empathy	Mutual Respect	

2. Unhealthy relationships involve

Blame	Insecurity	Submissions
Control	Jealousy	Sulking
Dishonesty	Manipulation	Victims
Fear	Perpetrators	Withdrawal
Guilt	Put-downs	Win/lose results
Harassment	Sexism	

Name six of the most important friendships in your life and list the descriptors that characterize your relationship with each person.

Name   **Characteristics**

1. _____   _____
2. _____   _____
3. _____   _____
4. _____   _____
5. _____   _____
6. _____   _____

Which of your relationships support healthy self-esteem and feelings of empowerment?

_____

_____

Which of your relationships contribute to low self-esteem and feelings of discouragement?

_____

_____

How do you plan to deal with those relationships that are destructive to your emotional well-being?

_____

_____

How do you encourage the positive relationships in your life?

_____

_____

One way to handle destructive relationships, which tear down your self-esteem, is to respond to criticism, put-downs, and harassing remarks with assertive statements. The following are some ways to respond to disrespectful comments:

"I" statements:	"I feel extremely hurt when you speak to me that way."
It bugs me:	"It bugs me when you disrespect me that way. I wish you would stop."
Call it like it is:	"That's harassment, and harassment is against the school policy."
Say what you will do:	"If this harassment continues, I will have to report it to the school administration."
Say something crazy:	"Purple kumquat!"

Remember, you don't have to stay in an unhealthy, destructive friendship; you are able to choose your friends based on mutual admiration and respect. The sooner you are able establish positive relationships in your life, the sooner you will begin to admire and respect yourself and begin to build healthy self-esteem. Harassment and put-downs are common in unhealthy relationships. When someone tries to pull you down by making a negative remark, use one of the responses from the preceding list and move away from that person. Hang out with positive people; you will find that you will become much happier and more positive yourself.

The next time someone is disrespectful to me, I will say

_____

or _____

If that doesn't work, I will

_____

or _____

WE EACH HAVE FAMILY NEEDS

GOALS OF THE EXERCISE

1. Verbalize specific support given by the family.
2. List personal needs required from the family.
3. Identify the personal contributions that can be made to the family.
4. Recognize the needs and contributions of other family members.

ADDITIONAL PROBLEMS FOR WHICH THIS EXERCISE MAY BE MOST USEFUL

- Attention-Seeking Behavior
- Blended Family
- Divorce
- Parenting Skills/Discipline
- Responsible Behavior Training

SUGGESTIONS FOR USING THIS EXERCISE WITH STUDENT(S)

Students who deal with sibling rivalry may view the process of getting their needs met as a one-way street where they demand and another family member either does or does not provide. This point of view interprets the family resources as finite and only able to accommodate a limited number of needs. The activity is designed to help the student redefine the family resources in terms of the needs and contributions of each of its members. The family resources become much greater when each family member shares in the overall task of providing for the group as a whole. This perception of giving and getting helps the student assume a cooperative rather than a competitive attitude toward participation in the family unit.

The activity can be completed by the student alone or during an individual or group counseling session. Once completed, it should be processed with the counselor and also with the parents if appropriate. This activity is appropriate for students in grades 4 through 12 and with younger students if assistance is given.

WE EACH HAVE FAMILY NEEDS

Each of us has basic needs that ideally are provided by our families. Basic needs include food, shelter, love, relationships, and learning how to survive. Many families also provide additional support (e.g., financial assistance, transportation, food preparation, skill development). The following is a list of ways that families accommodate their members. Read the list, adding some additional ideas of your own. Remember that every family provides for some of these needs, but no family provides them all.

Active listening	Empathy	Protection
Advice	Extended friendships	Pride
Allowance	Family get-togethers	Responsibility training
Attention	Financial support	School supplies
Birthday celebrations	Food	Skill development
Character training	Food preparation	Sports equipment
Child care	Games	Time
Church affiliation	Homework support	Toys
Clothing	Housecleaning	Transportation
Community associations	Hugs	Vacations
Educational support	Love	Volunteer work
Entertainment	Problem solving	Yard work

Now add some ideas of your own:

_____   _____   _____

_____   _____   _____

List some of the important resources that you get from your family; then list the resources and support that you can give back to your family to help keep the family resource bank full. Families function best when each member contributes to make sure that the needs of all are met.

Resources I Need From My Family

_____
_____
_____
_____
_____
_____

Resources I Can Contribute to My Family

_____
_____
_____
_____
_____
_____

Others in your family require support from the family resources and contribute back into the resource bank as well. List the resources needed by your parents, siblings, and other family members.

Resources Needed by My Mother

_____
_____
_____
_____
_____

Resources Contributed by My Mother

_____
_____
_____
_____
_____

Resources Needed by My Father

_____
_____
_____
_____

Resources Contributed by My Father

_____
_____
_____
_____

Resources Needed by My Sibling

_____
_____
_____
_____

Resources Contributed by My Sibling

_____
_____
_____
_____

Resources Needed by _____

_____
_____
_____
_____
_____

Resources Contributed by _____

_____
_____
_____
_____
_____

Resources Needed by _____

_____
_____
_____
_____
_____

Resources Contributed by _____

_____
_____
_____
_____
_____

Resources Needed by _____

_____
_____
_____
_____
_____

Resources Contributed by _____

_____
_____
_____
_____
_____

SIBLING RELATIONSHIPS: AN AMAZING EVOLUTION

GOALS OF THE EXERCISE

1. Establish a more positive relationship with siblings.
2. Recognize that sibling relationships evolve over time.
3. Identify ways to improve current sibling relationships.
4. Imagine sibling relationships in the future.

ADDITIONAL PROBLEMS FOR WHICH THIS EXERCISE MAY BE MOST USEFUL

- Attention-Seeking Behavior
- Blended Family
- Conflict Management
- Divorce
- Parenting Skills/Discipline

SUGGESTIONS FOR USING THIS EXERCISE WITH STUDENT(S)

Students who view their siblings as rivals or potential threats to their happiness and status in the home often neglect to recognize the long-term benefits of having siblings. The Sibling Relationships: An Amazing Evolution activity allows the student to picture his or her relationships with siblings as evolving over a lifetime. The student is asked first to describe the current relationship with his or her siblings and then to interview older people of various ages to determine how sibling relationships change. The results of the interviews are then recorded on the activity sheet. After interviewing a teen, an adult, a grandparent, and a great-grandparent to determine how people in various age brackets feel about their siblings, the student is instructed to predict his or her own relationships with siblings in the years to come. Finally, the student is directed to state the many positive aspects of having the love and support of siblings as he or she proceeds through life and to identify some strategies for improving current sibling relationships.

The student can interview people from his or her own family, school, church, or community. If the student has difficulty finding people willing to discuss their sibling relationships, the counselor can arrange to have someone from each age category visit the individual or group counseling session and address the issue. This activity is appropriate for students in grades 3 through 8.

SIBLING RELATIONSHIPS: AN AMAZING EVOLUTION

Name: _____ **Age:** _____ **Date:** _____

Your relationship with your siblings begins when you are quite young and will probably extend throughout most of your lifetime. During that time, your feelings for each other will evolve and change many times. Describe your relationship with your siblings now. Include what you appreciate and don't appreciate about each one of your brothers and sisters.

Things I appreciate about _____ , _____ , _____ , _____ (names and ages of your siblings):

_____

_____

_____

_____

Things I don't appreciate about my siblings:

_____

_____

_____

_____

To imagine how you and your siblings will get along in the future, interview some people who are older than you and ask them about their relationship with their siblings. Interview a teen and three adults—one your parent's age, one your grandparent's age, and one who is a great-grandparent—to find out what kind of relationship they have with their siblings today. Report your findings on the lines provided.

Name of the teen you interviewed: _____

Positive comments the teen has about his or her sibling relationships:

_____

_____

Negative comments this person has about his or her sibling relationships:

_____

_____

Name of the adult of your parent's age you interviewed: _____

Positive comments this person has about his or her sibling relationships:

_____

_____

Negative comments this person has about his or her sibling relationships:

_____

_____

Name of the adult of your grandparent's age you interviewed: _____

Positive comments this person has about his or her sibling relationships:

_____

_____

Negative comments this person has about his or her sibling relationships:

_____

_____

Name of the great-grandparent you interviewed: _____

Positive comments this person has about his or her sibling relationships:

_____

_____

Negative comments this person has about his or her sibling relationships:

_____

_____

Based on your interviews, how do you think your relationship with your siblings will change?

As a teen, I will probably have the following feelings about my siblings:

_____

_____

As an adult, I will probably have the following feelings about my siblings:

_____

_____

As a grandparent, I will probably have the following feelings about my siblings:

_____

_____

As a great-grandparent, I will probably have the following feelings about my siblings:

_____

_____

The best thing about having siblings for a lifetime is:

_____

_____

_____

_____

_____

_____

_____

_____

_____

Things I can do right now to improve my relationship with my siblings:

_____

_____

_____

_____

_____

_____

_____

_____

_____

_____

_____

_____

_____

RECIPES FOR RESTITUTION

GOALS OF THE EXERCISE

1. Express remorse for problems caused for others.
2. Acknowledge the importance of making restitution for thoughtless behavior.
3. Identify various methods to remedy mistakes.
4. Identify personal mistakes that require restitution.

ADDITIONAL PROBLEMS FOR WHICH THIS EXERCISE MAY BE MOST USEFUL

- Anger Management/Aggression
- Attachment/Bonding Deficits
- Attention-Seeking Behavior
- Conflict Management
- Parenting Skills/Discipline

SUGGESTIONS FOR USING THIS EXERCISE WITH STUDENT(S)

Mistakes are a normal part of living. However, some mistakes create distress, hurt, frustration, or extra work for others. When actions create problems for someone else, it is important to make restitution for the damage done. There are many ways to remedy an affront to another. The Recipes for Restitution activity lists various remedies and asks the student to brainstorm several more ideas and record them on the worksheet.

Examples of offending mistakes and possible remedies are provided on the worksheet. The student is instructed to record two personal mistakes and determine an appropriate gesture of restitution for each. These two Recipes for Restitution can be done during a counseling session to ensure that the student correctly identifies an appropriate remedy for a problem he or she has caused. The student is then asked to record the mistakes made in the subsequent two weeks and devise a plan of restitution for each. After the plan has been implemented, the student is instructed to draw or place a star beside the Restitution line to congratulate him- or herself for the completed effort. This activity is appropriate for students in grades 3 through 12 and can be modified for use with younger students.

RECIPES FOR RESTITUTION

Everyone occasionally behaves in a manner that causes problems for others. Our thoughtless actions can hurt another person's feelings, damage personal belongings, or interfere with important plans. There are many ways to apologize or remedy a mistake that has offended or created a hardship for another person. Read the list of ways you can make restitution for a problem you have caused and brainstorm some additional ideas of your own.

Apologize in person	Make up the work	_____
Apologize on the phone	Pay for the damage	_____
Ask, "How can I help?"	Replace damaged object	_____
Clean up	Rewind your behavior (see "The Rewind Game")	_____
Do a favor		_____
Do extra chores	Rewind your words	_____
Draw a picture	Send flowers	_____
Include in a game or activity	Share a treat	_____
Listen to upset feelings	Use an "I" statement	_____
Make something	Write a note	_____

Record on the following lines some mistakes you have made, and write a remedy or a gesture of restitution that would help make up for the hurt feelings or problems caused to another person. You may use one or a combination of the remedies from the preceding list.

Example
Thoughtless behavior: I forgot to take the cookies out of the oven like I promised my mom I would. They were burned so badly that we couldn't eat them.
Restitution: I made another batch of cookies and watched them closely so they would turn out perfect.

Thoughtless behavior: I told my friend that I would play with him at recess, but I played soccer instead. His feelings were hurt.

Restitution: I apologized to my friend and asked if I could make it up to him by playing with him during the next two recesses. He said OK and accepted my apology.

Thoughtless behavior: _____

_____

Restitution: _____

_____

Thoughtless behavior: _____

_____

Restitution: _____

_____

Record during the next two weeks the mistakes you make that negatively affect another person. Write down how you plan to make restitution, and follow through with your idea. After you have remedied the problem, place a star next to the Restitution line to congratulate yourself for the completed effort.

Thoughtless behavior: _____

_____

Restitution: _____

_____

Thoughtless behavior: _____

_____

Restitution: _____

_____

Thoughtless behavior: _____

_____

Restitution: _____

_____

Thoughtless behavior: _____

_____

Restitution: _____

_____

Thoughtless behavior: _____

_____

Restitution: _____

_____

Thoughtless behavior: _____

_____

Restitution: _____

_____

RECORD OF BEHAVIORAL PROGRESS

GOALS OF THE EXERCISE

1. Identify the student's inappropriate behavior.
2. Determine the factors that reinforce the student's negative behavior.
3. Identify the mistaken goals of the student's misbehavior.
4. Plan interventions that will encourage and reinforce the student's appropriate behavior.

ADDITIONAL PROBLEMS FOR WHICH THIS EXERCISE MAY BE MOST USEFUL

*   Assessment for Special Services
*   Attention-Seeking Behavior
*   Career Planning
*   Physical Disabilities
*   Bullying Perpetrator

SUGGESTIONS FOR USING THIS EXERCISE WITH STUDENT(S)

The Record of Behavioral Progress is to be used by the counselor, social worker, parents, Multidisciplinary Evaluation Team (MET), or educators who seek to evaluate the student's inappropriate or dysfunctional behavior and plan for specific intervention strategies that will help him/her develop positive alternative behaviors. The Record of Behavioral Progress is useful in preparing for child study meetings, MET meetings, and IEPC meetings, as well as for determining how to redirect a student who uses negative rather than positive methods to meet his or her basic needs. This activity is appropriate for students in all grade levels.

INSTRUCTIONS FOR USING THE RECORD OF BEHAVIORAL PROGRESS TO EVALUATE STUDENTS' BEHAVIOR

Begin by listing the behaviors of concern in column 1. Use specific descriptors (e.g., hitting, out of seat, interrupting, incomplete homework) rather than generalizations (e.g., inattention, rudeness, poor study habits). Complete column 2 by listing all possible factors that may be encouraging the inappropriate behavior. These will be reactions from parents and other family members, teachers, educational specialists, paraeducators, and peers that reinforce the negative actions of the student. Then use column 3 to identify the student's mistaken goals of misbehavior or the reward he or she seeks by engaging in the negative behavior (e.g., attention, power, revenge, or fear of failure); see *Children: The Challenge* by Dreikurs.

Plan for intervention strategies by considering the goals of the student's misbehavior and determining how to help him or her meet these goals with the use of positive rather than negative behavior. If the student is seeking attention, how can his or her needs be met through cooperative, socially appropriate, and productive behavior? List some techniques of positive discipline (e.g., consequences, encouragement, choices, enforceable limits, "I" statements) in column 4 that will encourage the student's positive behavior and eliminate the reinforcement of the existing negative behavior. Describe the outcome of the interventions in column 5. Keep an ongoing record of the strategies that do and do not work and revise the planned interventions as needed.

RECORD OF BEHAVIORAL PROGRESS

Date: _____

Student: _____   Age or grade: _____

Consultant (parent, teacher, or educational specialist): _____

1. Negative Behavior	2. Negative Behavior Reinforcement Factors	3. Child's Goal(s)	4. Planned Interventions	5. Outcomes

ART OF CREATING AND MAINTAINING FRIENDSHIPS

GOALS OF THE EXERCISE

1. Identify the essential ingredients for making and keeping friends.
2. Discuss friendship skills in a group or with the counselor.
3. Develop more positive social skills.
4. Choose one friendship skill to work on personally.

ADDITIONAL PROBLEMS FOR WHICH THIS EXERCISE MAY BE MOST USEFUL

- Anger Management/Aggression
- Conflict Management
- Parenting Skills/Discipline
- School Refusal/Phobia
- Self-Esteem Building

SUGGESTIONS FOR USING THIS EXERCISE WITH STUDENT(S)

The Art of Creating and Maintaining Friendships activity allows the student to consider the essential ingredients of being a friend by working on a word search puzzle. Twenty-four friendship skills are listed and included in the puzzle. The listed skills are to be discussed in a group or with the counselor individually before the puzzle is attempted to ensure that the student is familiar with each technique. Some of the skills are quite obvious (e.g., play, laugh, help, share), whereas others may need defining (e.g., compromise, empathy, appreciate).

Ask the student to work on the puzzle alone, with his or her parents, or during the social skills group. If done in a group, the students can race one another or the counselor and then help others to find the elusive words. The purpose of the activity is to familiarize the student with the techniques necessary for social maturity and friendship building. The student is asked to list some additional strategies that are useful for creating and maintaining friendships. After additional strategies have been brainstormed, the student is directed to name the skill he or she considers most important personally and to describe why. A puzzle key is provided at the end of the activity. This activity is appropriate for students in grades 3 through 12.

ART OF CREATING AND MAINTAINING FRIENDSHIPS

The following is a list of ingredients that are important when trying to make or keep friends. Read the list over and ask your parent, teacher, or counselor to explain any of the friendship skills you aren't sure about or discuss how each ingredient promotes friendships in your social skills group.

Accept	Forgive	Put-ups
Activities	Fun	Share
Apologize	Give and take	Smile
Appreciate	Help	Stick up for
Common interests	Include	Support
Compromise	Laugh	Take turns
Empathy	Listen	Talk
Encourage	Play together	Understand

Solve the following word puzzle by finding all the friendship words of the preceding list.

Friendship Skills

```
E  R  A  H  S  Y  H  T  A  P  M  E  S  Z  S
G  E  T  A  I  C  E  R  P  P  A  V  P  T  A
D  I  Y  L  A  C  C  E  P  T  J  A  S  A  C
B  E  V  Q  I  F  U  N  N  B  A  E  X  P  T
U  N  D  E  R  S  T  A  N  D  R  H  X  P  I
E  O  P  L  A  Y  T  O  G  E  T  H  E  R  V
N  S  J  A  K  N  L  E  T  E  T  O  D  O  I
C  O  I  L  P  A  D  N  N  A  Y  T  U  F  T
O  E  A  M  U  O  I  T  K  V  R  P  L  P  I
U  T  V  G  O  N  L  E  A  O  P  U  C  U  E
R  E  H  I  O  R  T  O  P  K  L  T  N  K  S
A  O  L  M  G  U  P  P  G  T  E  U  I  C  Z
G  D  M  I  R  R  U  M  T  I  H  P  K  I  B
E  O  J  N  M  S  O  Z  O  G  Z  S  B  T  Y
C  A  S  A  O  S  P  F  Q  C  Z  E  X  S  Q
```

Add a few more friendship skills that aren't listed.

_____   _____   _____

_____   _____   _____

_____   _____   _____

Which ingredient do you think is most important for you to make and keep friends?
_____ Why? _____

_____

```
                          Solution
    E  R  A  H  S  Y  H  T  A  P  M  E  +  +  S
    G  E  T  A  I  C  E  R  P  P  A  +  +  T  A
    +  I  +  L  A  C  C  E  P  T  +  +  S  +  C
    +  +  V  +  I  F  U  N  +  +  +  E  +  +  T
    U  N  D  E  R  S  T  A  N  D  R  +  +  +  I
    E  +  P  L  A  Y  T  O  G  E  T  H  E  R  V
    N  S  +  A  K  N  L  E  T  +  T  +  D  O  I
    C  +  I  L  P  A  D  N  N  A  +  T  U  F  T
    O  E  A  M  U  O  I  T  K  +  R  P  L  P  I
    U  T  V  G  O  N  L  E  A  O  P  U  C  U  E
    R  E  H  I  O  R  T  O  P  K  L  T  N  K  S
    A  +  L  M  G  U  P  P  G  +  E  U  I  C  +
    G  +  M  I  R  R  U  M  +  I  H  P  +  I  +
    E  O  +  N  M  S  O  +  O  +  Z  S  +  T  +
    C  +  S  +  +  S  +  F  +  C  +  E  +  S  +
```

(Over, Down, Direction):

ACCEPT (5, 3, E)   INCLUDE (13, 12, N)
ACTIVITIES (15, 2, S)   LAUGH (7, 7, SW)
APOLOGIZE (4, 7, SE)   LISTEN (4, 3, SE)
APPRECIATE (11, 2, W)   PLAY TOGETHER (3, 6, E)
COMMON INTERESTS (1, 15, NE)   PUT-UPS (12, 9, S)
COMPROMISE (10, 15, NW)   SHARE (5, 1, W)
EMPATHY (12, 1, W)   SMILE (6, 15, NW)
ENCOURAGE (1, 6, S)   STICK UP FOR (14, 15, N)
FORGIVE (8, 15, NW)   SUPPORT (6, 14, NE)
FUN (6, 4, E)   TAKE TURNS (11, 7, SW)
GIVE AND TAKE (1, 2, SE)   TALK (2, 10, NE)
HELP (11, 13, N)   UNDERSTAND (1, 5, E)

WIN/WIN VERSUS WIN/LOSE

GOALS OF THE EXERCISE

1. Understand the benefits of consensus problem solving.
2. Differentiate between win/win and win/lose solutions.
3. Improve interpersonal problem-solving skills.
4. Learn methods of solving interpersonal conflict fairly and positively.

ADDITIONAL PROBLEMS FOR WHICH THIS EXERCISE MAY BE MOST USEFUL

- Anger Management/Aggression
- Attachment/Bonding Deficits
- Conflict Management
- Responsible Behavior Training

SUGGESTIONS FOR USING THIS EXERCISE WITH STUDENT(S)

Achieving compromise and consensus are social skills that students can learn at a very early age and should continue to refine throughout their lifetime. The Win/Win Versus Win/Lose activity explains the benefits of working toward a mutually acceptable solution when faced with a dispute or different points of view. Several examples of win/win and win/lose settlements are provided, and the student is instructed to write additional scenarios from his or her own experience. This exercise can be used individually with the student or completed in a group setting. The student is then directed to draw a picture of a win/win and a win/lose solution and to indicate which type of problem solving he or she will use next time a dispute arises. This activity is appropriate for students in grades 1 through 6.

WIN/WIN VERSUS WIN/LOSE

When you have a conflict or a point of view different from that of your friend's, it is best to work out the difference with a compromise that satisfies both of you. This is called a *win/win solution*. Win/win solutions develop problem-solving skills and build friendships. Students who choose a win/win approach find that others enjoy spending time with them, are willing to cooperate with them, and admire their ability to settle disputes fairly.

Other types of settlements result in negative feelings and lack of cooperation. A *win/lose solution* satisfies one person but not the other, and a *lose/lose solution* satisfies no one. These settlements create rebellion, frustration, and antagonism. Some win/win and win/lose solutions are given in the following list. Read these examples and describe a couple from your own experience. When you finish with your examples, draw a picture of one win/win result and one win/lose result.

Example

Win/Win	**Win/Lose**
Jimmy and Janice each want to draw with a set of crayons. They decide to share them so that they can each draw.	*Jimmy and Janice each want to draw with a set of crayons. Jimmy gets the box first and decides not to share.*
Several students want to jump rope at recess time. The group decides to rotate the jumpers and twirlers.	*Several students want to jump rope at recess time. Three students get the jump rope first and tell the others to find their own jump rope.*
Fred and his friends let Jerome join their soccer game, even though Jerome hasn't played the game much. They know he will learn as he plays.	*Fred and his friends tell Jerome that he will have to become a better soccer player before he can play with them.*

Now list some examples of your own:

Win/Win   **Win/Lose**

_____   _____

_____   _____

_____   _____

Win/Win   **Win/Lose**

_____   _____

_____   _____

_____   _____

_____   _____

_____   _____

Draw a picture of a win/win solution that satisfied both parties:

Draw a picture of a win/lose or lose/lose situation that resulted in frustration and upset feelings for one or both parties:

Next time I'm involved in a dispute or a difference of opinion, I will work for a _____ _____ solution, because _____

_____

_____

ANTIDOTES TO RELAPSE

GOALS OF THE EXERCISE

1. Define threats to recovery.
2. Identify antidotes to prevent a relapse of substance abuse.
3. Define a plan for recovery.
4. Abstain from substance abuse.

ADDITIONAL PROBLEMS FOR WHICH THIS EXERCISE MAY BE MOST USEFUL

- Parenting Skills/Discipline
- Physical/Sexual Abuse
- Responsible Behavior Training
- Sexual Responsibility
- Suicide Ideation/Attempt
- Teen Pregnancy

SUGGESTIONS FOR USING THIS EXERCISE WITH STUDENT(S)

The road to recovery is long and hard for students who have become addicted to substances. The Antidotes to Relapse activity is designed to help the student recognize the healthy habits that can avert temptations and promote a substance-free lifestyle. Numerous healthy habits and behaviors are listed that can support the student's commitment to remain substance-free. The student is asked to add some additional actions that can defend against the pull of addiction and related behaviors. The student is reminded that giving up an unhealthy habit is nearly impossible unless he or she substitutes it with a healthy habit.

After reviewing the Antidotes to Relapse list, the student is instructed to define some personal temptations or danger zones and to choose a healthy habit that will resist a relapse to addictive behavior. The student is then asked to identify the most helpful strategy, a person to turn to for support, and the major reason he or she is committed to recovery. This activity can be used repeatedly as the student progresses toward the goal of remaining substance-free. It is appropriate for students in all grade levels who struggle with addiction.

ANTIDOTES TO RELAPSE

There are many antidotes to help you prevent a relapse to chemical dependence. Experienced support systems exist to guide you in your journey toward recovery. These include your family and school, religious groups, and community agencies, all of which are willing and able to offer the love, encouragement, and guidance that you need. The most important resource you have is yourself. Once you determine that you want to live a substance-free lifestyle, you will discover that others are anxious to offer real assistance. The following is a list of positive habits and behaviors that will greatly assist you in your efforts to remain substance-free. Addiction comprises an extremely dangerous set of behaviors that will eventually take over your life if they are not defeated. The best way to stop a bad habit is to replace it with a positive habit. Read the following list and determine which positive actions you can begin taking today:

Accept the support of others who care

Admit to your abuse and talk about it with your parents and counselor

Agree to drug screening

Attend religious services

Commit to recovery

Consider the future

Cooperate with family counseling

Develop a plan for recovery

Develop a substance-free hobby

Draw

Encourage others to be substance-free

Follow the instructions of your doctor

Forgive the past

Get a chemical dependence evaluation

Get counseling

Hang out with substance-free friends

Help others

Identify temptations for relapse

Improve school attendance

Join a school-sponsored club

Join a support group

Keep a journal

Know the facts about addiction and substance abuse

Learn anger management

Listen to the concerns of others

Play a sport

Read recovery literature

Sign a contract for substance-free living

Verbalize the destructive nature of chemical dependence

Work out or exercise

Write your addiction story

Write your recovery story

Add several antidotes of your own:

_____   _____

_____   _____

_____   _____

_____   _____

_____   _____

Identify several of your danger zones or temptations for relapse and choose an antidote that will help you keep your commitment to remain substance-free.

Example

Problem	**Antidote**
• *My old friends who drink and use drugs invite me to a party.*	• *I decide to do something with my substance-free friends instead.*
• *I am tempted to skip school and get high.*	• *I talk to my counselor and commit to improve my attendance one day at a time.*

• _____   • _____

• _____   • _____

• _____   • _____

• _____   • _____

• _____   • _____

• _____   • _____

• _____   • _____

My most helpful strategy is _____

The person I can turn to for support is _____

The biggest reason I want to continue my recovery is _____

_____

Name: _____

Date: _____

MY CONTRACT FOR A SUBSTANCE-FREE LIFESTYLE

GOALS OF THE EXERCISE

1. Commit to abstaining from substance usage.
2. Identify a personal support system.
3. Commit to asking for help when tempted to relapse.
4. Plan for long-term abstinence from mind-altering substances.

ADDITIONAL PROBLEMS FOR WHICH THIS EXERCISE MAY BE MOST USEFUL

- Parenting Skills/Discipline
- Physical/Sexual Abuse
- Responsible Behavior Training
- Sexual Responsibility
- Suicide Ideation/Attempt
- Teen Pregnancy

SUGGESTIONS FOR USING THIS EXERCISE WITH STUDENT(S)

In the My Contract for a Substance-Free Lifestyle activity, the student is asked to sign a contract committing to abstinence from mind-altering substances and to successfully contact supportive people or agencies in the event of a desire to relapse. The contract worksheet reminds the student that many supportive people and agencies are willing to provide time, encouragement, and resources to help him or her through the difficult stages of recovery. However, recovery cannot begin without a committed intention to refrain from using addictive substances.

Read the contract out loud and encourage the student to sign and date it. The parents, counselor, and/or teacher are also requested to sign the document. Included in the document is a statement that the parents and supportive others agree to contact the counselor or therapist if, in their view, the student is in danger of relapse. Have the student complete the names and phone numbers of people and agencies that he or she agrees to contact immediately in times of crisis.

Congratulate the student for signing the contract, and join the parents in confirming a willingness to support the student's efforts to fight substance addiction. Caution the parents to remain vigilant for any signs of relapse. Although a refusal to sign the contract indicates a desire for continued substance abuse, a signed contract does not guarantee abstinence without relapse. The contract is only an initial step in the fight against addiction. This activity is appropriate for students of any age who are struggling with substance abuse.

MY CONTRACT FOR A SUBSTANCE-FREE LIFESTYLE

You are not alone. People who care about you want you to remain substance-free and want to help you with your recovery. You are your greatest resource. Your personal control over substance abuse begins with your commitment to abstain from the use of any form of mind-altering substances. Once you have made that commitment, you can count on the love and encouragement of others to support you in your efforts to overcome your addiction. Fill out and sign the contract below to commit to maintaining a substance-free lifestyle.

CONTRACT FOR A SUBSTANCE-FREE LIFESTYLE

I, _____ agree that I will not use mind-altering substances of any nature.

   I, _____ further agree that if and when I sense any danger of a relapse or desire to use a restricted substance, I will successfully contact at least one of the people listed below to help me to resist the temptation and honor my commitment to remain substance-free.

   I understand that should my parents or any significant other suspect that I am in danger of a relapse, they are obligated to contact my counselor or therapist immediately.

Signed: _____   _____
              Student   Parent

_____   _____
   Teacher or Counselor   Parent

Date: _____

Individuals or agencies to call for help and support: Phone numbers:

Mother: _____   Home: _____   Other: _____

Father: _____   Home: _____   Other: _____

Therapist: _____   Work: _____   Other: _____

Counselor: _____   Work: _____   Other: _____

Substance Abuse Hotline: _____   Phone: _____

Emergency Room: _____   Phone: _____

Police or Sheriff: _____ Phone: _____

Supportive Other: _____ Home: _____ Other: _____

Supportive Other: _____ Home: _____ Other: _____

Supportive Other: _____ Home: _____ Other: _____

Supportive Other: _____ Home: _____ Other: _____

HEART-TO-HEART SMART TALKS

GOALS OF THE EXERCISE

1. Schedule regular appointments for student/parent communication.
2. Learn rules for effective communication.
3. Maintain a supportive and loving parent/child relationship.
4. Student and parents gain a better understanding of one another's point of view.

ADDITIONAL PROBLEMS FOR WHICH THIS EXERCISE MAY BE MOST USEFUL

- Anger Management/Aggression
- Attention-Seeking Behavior
- Conflict Management
- Parenting Skills/Discipline
- Self-Esteem Building

SUGGESTIONS FOR USING THIS EXERCISE WITH STUDENT(S)

Students who are depressed or in other critically emotional states often stop communicating with their parents and others at a time when they vitally need the love and support of those who care. The communication that does take place frequently ends in heated differences, lack of understanding, and extreme frustration. The Heart-to-Heart Smart Talks activity emphasizes the importance of effective communication for both parents and the student. It leads the parent and student through the process of making time for productive and supportive emotional expression on an ongoing basis. The activity is designed to be completed by the student together with his/her parent or parents.

A heart-to-heart smart talk is defined as an arranged conversation in which positive communication techniques are used to ensure that the ideas of both parties are expressed and heard. The rules for a heart-to-heart smart talk are outlined, and a list of typical times when parents and students can get together to talk is given. Both parents and students are instructed to add some additional time slots of when they can meet, and both are asked to respond to some considerations that will help them prepare for their first heart-to-heart smart talk. They are directed to set the date for the first meeting and to sign and date the document. The list of considerations can be used repeatedly by the student and the parent to ensure that the keys to effective communication are being observed. This activity is appropriate for students in grades 6 through 12.

HEART-TO-HEART SMART TALKS
(FOR STUDENTS AND PARENTS)

Communication is a key element in any parent/child relationship. Effective communication becomes vital during emotionally volatile times of personal or family crisis. The expression of personal feelings and listening nonjudgmentally and empathically is one of the greatest gifts that parents and students can give to one another. Reserving a regular time for sharing feelings, concerns, ideas, plans, hopes, and dreams will strengthen the relationship and develop a loving support system that enhances self-esteem and reduces anxiety and depression for both the parent and the student.

A *heart-to-heart smart talk* is an arranged conversation in which positive communication techniques are used to ensure that the ideas of both parties are expressed and heard.

The following are the rules for heart-to-heart smart talks:

1. Select a time to talk privately that is convenient for both the parent and the student.
2. Any topic is okay to bring up.
3. It is okay to say "pass" or "not right now" when a topic becomes too uncomfortable.
4. Use active listening (e.g., listening nonjudgmentally and empathically).
5. Use "I" messages (e.g., "I feel . . . when . . . because . . . ") as a way to express feelings and reactions without blaming the other person.
6. The purpose of a heart-to-heart smart talk is to understand the other person better, not to try to make him or her do something.
7. Before concluding, agree on a mutually acceptable time for your next heart-to-heart smart talk.

The following is a list of typical times that students and their parents can get together for a heart-to-heart smart talk. Read over the list and add some additional time slots of your own.

After school	Breakfast	Scheduled appointment
After work	Dinner	Sharing a soft drink
After dinner	Family meetings	Shopping
Before bedtime	In the car	Taking a walk
Before school	Lunch	Working together

Additional Times From the Parent(s)   Additional Times From the Student

_____   _____

_____   _____

_____   _____

_____   _____

Now respond to some considerations that will help you prepare for your next heart-to-heart smart talk.

Active listening means that I will

Parent's response: _____

_____

Student's response: _____

_____

Keys to expressing my opinion are

Parent's response: _____

_____

Student's response: _____

_____

Some concerns my child has are

Parent's response: _____

_____

Some concerns my parent has are

Student's response: _____

_____

Some concerns I have are

Parent's response: _____

_____

Some concerns I have are

Student's response: _____

_____

Scheduled time for the next heart-to-heart smart talk: _____

Student's signature: _____

Parent's signature: _____

Date: _____

ASSIGNMENT COMPLETION WORKSHEET

GOALS OF THE EXERCISE

1. Assume responsibility for daily academic assignments.
2. Schedule the study time necessary to complete assignments.
3. Organize and plan for success in school.
4. Evaluate the weekly rate of assignment completion.

ADDITIONAL PROBLEMS FOR WHICH THIS EXERCISE MAY BE MOST USEFUL

- Academic Motivation
- Attention-Seeking Behavior
- Divorce
- Depression
- Self-Esteem Building
- Suicide Ideation/Attempt

SUGGESTIONS FOR USING THIS EXERCISE WITH STUDENT(S)

Depressed students sometimes feel that their lack of energy and demanding schedules prevent them from fulfilling their commitments and competing successfully in school. This can become a vicious circle of unfinished schoolwork, feeling unprepared and overwhelmed, and giving up and falling even farther behind. The student needs a method of organizing schoolwork and other activities and regaining confidence in his or her ability to succeed.

The Assignment Completion Worksheet helps the student plan for completing schoolwork by recording all assignments and designating a specific time to complete each project. Daily assignments are to be recorded by class and due date on the worksheet. The student is then instructed to complete an activity and assignment graph to determine when the work can be completed. The weekly assignment graph allows the student to review his or her schedule for the week and check the time available for additional activities. The student is directed to write all of his or her activities, commitments, and assignments on the graph in the appropriate time slots and check them off when they have been completed. Finally, the student can calculate the number of assignments completed for the week. The student is asked to rate his or her level of performance and to compare the level of productivity to the previous week's performance.

The graph will help the student keep track of how he or she spends time and will assist in developing time management skills. The process will empower the student to feel more in control of his or her schedule and life. Follow-up discussions should be held during counseling sessions, focusing on how the student is prioritizing and balancing his/her activities. This assignment is appropriate for students in grades 8 through 12.

ASSIGNMENT COMPLETION WORKSHEET

Name: _____ Grade: _____

Assignments for the week of _____ to _____ (day, month, year)

Planning and organizing your classroom and homework assignments, quizzes, tests, and projects for school is an essential key to academic success. This worksheet is designed to help you keep track of your assignments and find adequate time to complete them effectively and efficiently. By organizing your study time, you will feel more in control and confident about successfully participating in school. Take this worksheet with you to all of your classes; keep it in your planner if you have one. Record assignments next to the name of the class. Write in the due date when the assignment is given. When you have a break, write down the study times when you will work on the assignment. The weekly assignment graph at the end of this worksheet will help you determine when you have study time available.

Class	Assignments	Due Date	Study Times
Example:			
Algebra	*Chap. III, Pgs. 25–29*	*Wed.*	*Mon. 3:30–4:30, Tues. 3:30–4:30*
_____	_____	_____	_____
	_____	_____	_____
	_____	_____	_____
	_____	_____	_____
	_____	_____	_____
_____	_____	_____	_____
	_____	_____	_____
	_____	_____	_____
	_____	_____	_____
	_____	_____	_____

Class	Assignments	Due Date	Study Times

At the end of the week, determine how many assignments were successfully completed. Use the weekly assignment graph to help you assess your productivity.

This week I completed _____ of _____ assignments.

This is (check one) an improvement _____ or not as productive _____ when compared to last week's schoolwork.

I consider my study efforts this week to be (circle one):

    Poor   Fair   Good   Excellent!   Awesome!

My goal for next week is to _____
_____.

Signed: _____

Date: _____

Use the graph on the following page to schedule all of your assignments for this week. Block out unavailable times for schoolwork by shading in the squares with a colored pencil or marker and writing what you have scheduled for that time (e.g., lunch, basketball practice, chores, favorite TV program, sleep). Write the class name in the block representing the designated time for working on the assignment; for example, if you plan to work on algebra on Monday and Tuesday from 3:30 P.M. to 4:30 P.M., write "algebra" in those blocks. This graph will help you see at a glance the times you have available to complete your school assignments and other activities as well. After you have finished an assignment, check it off on the graph so that you can calculate the number of assignments completed for the week.

GRAPH OF MY WEEKLY ASSIGNMENTS

	Sun.	Mon.	Tues.	Wed.	Thurs.	Fri.	Sat.
2–3 A.M.							
1–2 A.M.							
12–1 A.M.							
11 P.M.–12 A.M.							
10–11 P.M.							
9–10 P.M.							
8–9 P.M.							
7–8 P.M.							
6–7 P.M.							
5–6 P.M.							
4–5 P.M.							
3–4 P.M.							
2–3 P.M.							
1–2 P.M.							
12–1 P.M.							
11 A.M.–12 P.M.							
10–11 A.M.							
9–10 A.M.							
8–9 A.M.							
7–8 A.M.							
6–7 A.M.							
5–6 A.M.							

LEGAL ASPECTS OF TEEN PARENTING

GOALS OF THE EXERCISE

1. Increase awareness of the legal issues of teen parenting.
2. Formulate a list of personal legal concerns.
3. Seek information regarding the legal aspects of teen parenting.
4. Develop a plan for addressing the legal issues of parenting.

ADDITIONAL PROBLEMS FOR WHICH THIS EXERCISE MAY BE MOST USEFUL

- Poverty/Economic Factors
- Responsible Behavior Training
- Self-Esteem Building
- Social Maladjustment/Conduct Disorder
- Social Skills/Peer Relationships
- Substance Abuse

SUGGESTIONS FOR USING THIS EXERCISE WITH STUDENT(S)

Many teen parents never consider the legal ramifications of their pregnancy. Much of the information they gather is from informal and sometimes uninformed sources, such as peers, family members, TV sitcoms, and videos. Many teen parents need accurate information that should be obtained from a professional who is familiar with county, state, and federal family laws. The Legal Aspects of Teen Pregnancy activity will help expectant teen parents prepare a list of legal questions before they seek advice from a lawyer, legal clinic, or family law specialist.

The most common legal issues facing teen parents are listed on the worksheet, along with the questions most typically asked. The student is asked to read over these topics and typical questions and highlight those of particular concern to him or her. This activity can be completed alone or by the coparents working together.

The student is then asked to formulate his or her own questions to prepare for a meeting with a legal advisor. The counselor or reproductive health teacher can address many of the questions in school; however, more complicated questions and issues should be referred to a legal advisor. The activity can help the student and counselor determine whether legal advice is necessary. The questions portion of the activity should be copied as often as necessary so that all of the student's questions can be recorded.

LEGAL ASPECTS OF TEEN PARENTING

There are many aspects of teen pregnancy that you may not have considered before you became pregnant. Some of your questions can be answered by your parents, teacher, or counselor. However, if you have legal questions concerning any of the following topics, you may want to consult with a legal clinic, a private lawyer, or a family law mediator.

Adoption

Child custody

Child support

Civil protective orders

Consent requirements

Domestic violence

Emancipation

Grandparents' rights

Informal guardianships

Juvenile dependency legal guardianships

Marriage license for minors

Physical or sexual abuse

Parental rights and responsibilities

Paternity

The court system

Unlawful sexual intercourse

Welfare for pregnant and parenting teens

Before you seek legal advice, it is wise to prepare a list of concerns that you and your coparent want to address. The following are some questions that pregnant teens typically ask:

1. What is adoption?
2. What are my options in addition to adoption?
3. What is the difference between physical and legal custody?
4. Can parents share custody?
5. Who is responsible for paying child support?
6. Can I continue going to school while I'm pregnant and after I have my baby?
7. How can we apply for a marriage license?
8. Do I qualify for welfare?
9. What are my rights and responsibilities as a parent?
10. How can I establish paternity?
11. What if my coparent doesn't want to help?
12. Did we break any laws by getting pregnant?
13. What should I do if abuse is involved?
14. What rights and responsibilities do my parents have?

Check or highlight any of these questions that are of particular interest to you. If you don't understand the topic behind a given question, ask your reproductive health teacher or counselor to define the topic and give you additional information. Then create a list of questions that you have about your pregnancy and any of the legal issues involved. You can start with the sample questions in the preceding list and then add your own more specific questions. Begin by getting information from your teacher or counselor and then decide if your situation requires more information from a legal counselor, a legal clinic, or a private lawyer. Use the Questions and Concerns about Our Pregnancy pages to formulate your questions. A topic of concern is the area you are wondering about (e.g., adoption, child custody, paternity, parents' rights and responsibilities). Make additional copies of these pages if necessary so that you can record all of your questions.

QUESTIONS AND CONCERNS ABOUT OUR PREGNANCY

Topic of concern: _____

My question: _____

_____

_____

Topic of concern: _____

My question: _____

_____

_____

Topic of concern: _____

My question: _____

_____

_____

Topic of concern: _____

My question: _____

_____

_____

Topic of concern: _____

My question: _____

_____

_____

Topic of concern: _____

My question: _____

_____

_____

GIVEN ANOTHER CHANCE, I'D MAKE A DIFFERENT CHOICE

GOALS OF THE EXERCISE

1. Verbalize the underlying causes of teen pregnancy.
2. Recognize how teen pregnancy can complicate a student's life.
3. Select healthier options for dealing with teen problems.
4. Commit to making positive choices about sexual responsibility in the future.

ADDITIONAL PROBLEMS FOR WHICH THIS EXERCISE MAY BE MOST USEFUL

- Poverty/Economic Factors
- Responsible Behavior Training
- Self-Esteem Building
- Social Maladjustment/Conduct Disorder
- Social Skills/Peer Relationships
- Substance Abuse

SUGGESTIONS FOR USING THIS EXERCISE WITH STUDENT(S)

The activity suggests to the student that teen pregnancy often occurs as the result of an attempt to solve an existing problem. However, rather than provide a solution, a baby often further complicates a teen's life. The activity presents several typical reasons given by teens for becoming pregnant, and the student is asked to list several personal reasons for making that choice. It is important that the student considers pregnancy as a choice that is under her control. Even if the teen did not intend to get pregnant, her decision to have unprotected sex was one with life-altering consequences. However, even though in the past the student may have made a poor choice that resulted in pregnancy, she will have many opportunities in the future to choose more wisely.

The activity provides examples of the way that pregnancy can complicate a teen's life. The student is instructed to consider this information and then write examples of how the decision to become pregnant has already complicated her life. Because pregnancy is often a choice made in an attempt to solve existing problems, the student is directed to a list of positive ways to solve problems that will simplify rather than further complicate her life. The student is then asked to indicate how she will solve problems in the future now that she has gained wisdom from her experiences. This activity is designed for students who have become pregnant; however, if the coparent is involved, he can also benefit from the information and questions in the exercise.

GIVEN ANOTHER CHANCE, I'D MAKE A DIFFERENT CHOICE

Teens often become pregnant because they want things to be different: They aren't satisfied with their current situation and believe that a baby can make their lives better. However, teen pregnancy is a long-term, labor-intensive solution to short-term problems. Usually, a baby only complicates a teen's life; instead of solving problems, becoming a parent can actually make things more difficult and frustrating. Many teen parents wish that they had made a different choice. They love their babies but wish they had waited until they were more settled and self-sufficient to become parents.

Some misguided reasons why teens get pregnant are the following:

Low self-esteem

Despair or pain resulting from

parental abuse or neglect

To create or accomplish

something of value

To have someone to love

Lack of a stable father figure

Lack of a stable mother figure

Family problems

To have someone to live for

To hold the boyfriend in the relationship

To have a family of their own

Desire to become emancipated

Social problems at school

Having friends who are pregnant

To stop going to school

To change their lives

Pressured into having sex

No clear goals for the future

List some of the personal reasons why you became pregnant:

_____   _____

_____   _____

The fact is that babies complicate the lives of teens by:
* Requiring an enormous amount of time and attention
* Interfering with continuing education and other goals
* Making it difficult to hold a job
* Making a social life nearly impossible

- Creating even more problems with a boyfriend
- Increasing the dependency on the teen's parents
- Causing sleep deprivation
- Leaving little time for personal activities

Add some of the complications that teen pregnancy has caused for you:

_____   _____

_____   _____

There are many ways to solve teen dilemmas that greatly improve the situation without requiring a lifelong commitment. Read the following list and select some suggestions that would work for you or add some additional ideas of your own on the lines provided.

Baby-sit	Get a job
Commit to abstinence or	Get counseling
birth control	Join a club at school
Create something beautiful	Postpone pregnancy until ready to
Find a boyfriend who	love, care for, and support a baby
agrees to wait for sex	Stay in school
Find a mentor	Improve the teen/parent relationship

_____   _____

_____   _____

_____   _____

It is never too late to start making good choices for yourself concerning sexual responsibility, pregnancy, and the kind of future you want for your family. There will always be problems in life, but the way you solve your problems is within your control. Experiencing a pregnancy can make you wiser and more capable of making positive choices in the future. You will have other chances to make different choices. Determine now what choices you will make. Think about the kind of future you want to create; then complete the following statements:

I am much wiser now because I have learned _____

_____

My biggest problem is _____

_____

I will solve this problem by _____

_____

If that doesn't work, I will _____

_____

Someone I can count on to help me with my problems is _____

Signed: _____ Date: _____

APPENDIX
ADDITIONAL ASSIGNMENTS
FOR PRESENTING PROBLEMS

ALPHABETICAL INDEX OF EXERCISES

ABOUT THE DOWNLOADABLE ASSIGNMENTS

Thank you for choosing the Wiley Practice*Planners*® series. *School Counseling and School Social Work Homework Planner, Second Edition's* website includes all the book's exercises in Word format for your convenience.

To access the assignments, please follow these steps:

Step 1 Go to www.wiley.com/go/hwpassignments

Step 2 Enter your email address, the password provided below, and click "submit"
Password: socialwork2017

Step 3 Select and download the listed exercises

If you need any assistance, please contact Wiley Customer Care 800-762-2974 (U.S.), 317-572-3994 (International) or visit www.wiley.com.